Deal Teams

Michael E.S. Frankel

Published by Aspatore, Inc.

For corrections, company/title updates, comments or any other inquiries, please e-mail info@aspatore.com.

First Printing, 2004

10 9 8 7 6 5 4 3 2 1

Copyright © 2004 by Aspatore, Inc. All rights reserved. Printed in the United States of America. No part of this publication may be reproduced or distributed in any form or by any means, or stored in a database or retrieval system, except as permitted under Sections 107 or 108 of the United States Copyright Act, without prior written permission of the publisher.

ISBN 1-58762-365-X Library of Congress Control Number: 2003116182

Material in this book is for educational purposes only. This book is sold with the understanding that neither any of the authors or the publisher is engaged in rendering medical, legal, accounting, investment, or any other professional service. For legal advice, please consult your personal lawyer.

This book is printed on acid free paper.

The views expressed by the individuals in this book do not necessarily reflect the views shared by the companies they are employed by (or the companies mentioned in this book).

About ASPATORE BOOKS – Publishers of C-Level Business Intelligence

www.Aspatore.com

Aspatore Books is the largest and most exclusive publisher of C-Level executives (CEO, CFO, CTO, CMO, Partner) from the world's most respected companies. Aspatore annually publishes a select group of C-Level executives from the Global 1,000, top 250 professional services firms, law firms (Partners & Chairs), and other leading companies of all sizes. C-Level Business Intelligence ™, as conceptualized and developed by Aspatore Books, provides professionals of all levels with proven business intelligence from industry insiders – direct and unfiltered insight from those who know it best – as opposed to third-party accounts offered by unknown authors and analysts. Aspatore Books is committed to publishing a highly innovative line of business books, and redefining such resources as indispensable tools for all professionals.

If you are a C-Level executive interested in submitting a manuscript to the Aspatore editorial board, please email jason@aspatore.com with the book idea, your biography, and any additional pertinent information.

Table of Contents

Acknowledgements

This book is the result of a year of writing, but also the result of a decade of deals. Over the course of my career I have closed dozens of transactions and worked on hundreds more. In every case I worked with colleagues and even counterparties from whom I learned much. My colleagues, clients and friends at Skadden, Arps, Merrill Lynch and VeriSign taught me a tremendous amount. To them I am indebted.

I would like to thank the staff at Aspatore for having faith in the project and working with me to bring it to fruition.

I would also like to thank my parents. Even before I began doing deals, I was learning the basic lessons of life from my mother and father, Professor Tamar Frankel and Professor Ernst Frankel. I would like to thank Shayna Klopott for her wise and tireless help turning gibberish into language. Without her, the book would be far worse at conveying thoughts to paper. Finally, I would like to thank Ben Cortopassi, my research assistant, who provided not only data to support my insights, but new insights of his own.

1

Introduction

A huge number of books have been written about mergers and acquisitions ("M&A"), divestitures, joint ventures, equity investments and alliances (together referred to as "Strategic Transactions" in this book). The most talented and sophisticated lawyers, accountants, investment bankers, consultants and CEOs have put pen to paper to share their thoughts about strategy, tactics, theory and practice. If you want to buy or sell a public or private company there is a huge literature to guide you in the process. But most of these books focus primarily, if not exclusively, on the buyer and seller as the sole dancers in this transactional tango; perhaps with the addition of a regulator in the background keeping the beat. However, as we all know, companies are just a legal façade beneath which lies a myriad of groups of people, each with different roles, objectives, goals and biases. Similarly, advisors to the companies are not just invisible support mechanisms but are also made up of individuals and have their own agendas and biases, both as organizations and individually. When we sit down at the deal table, we are faced with a variety of different people and organizations that together, make a deal happen. The process is driven not only by the goals of these people's organizations and their formal roles in them, but also by their personal and professional biases. Just as any baseball fan knows not only the stats of her favorite team, but the stats, and even personal quirks, of each player, understanding the deal means understanding all the players.

In this book, I try to peel back layers of the onion and discuss the people and organizations that sit within and beside the companies that buy and sell. I believe that understanding these people and organizations can help not only to get deals done, but to get them done well. This not only means extracting better terms from the other side, but also structuring terms that help both sides. One of the luxuries of doing Strategic Transactions is that they are not necessarily a net sum game. It is possible to create value for both sides – to increase the size of the pie – by understanding the players and their goals.

I will begin by discussing the buyer and seller themselves, as unified entities. The core of this book is premised on the idea that the individual players – the people – in a Strategic Transaction are the key to understanding the deal, but before you can understand the employees, it's important to understand the company for which they work and the way that entity is likely to behave based on economic and legal principals that drive it.

I will then peel back the legal façade and talk about the people that play roles within each of the buyer and seller. While a company may be guided by economic and legal forces, it is the people within the company that execute those goals. A company seeks to increase its stock price or grow its business, but it is individuals within the company that choose how best to execute those goals, and the devil is in the details. Therefore I will spend the majority of this book covering employees including executive management, line management and the corporate development team.

I will also cover various types of owners including institutional shareholders, founders and private investors. Employees make the day-to-day decisions, but always in theory and sometimes in practice, the owners have final say on the actions of a company.

I will also cover the board of directors that sits between these two groups. In many ways the board of directors is a hybrid of the two groups. They are more involved in the details of management than most investors but less so than employees. But they are tasked with representing the interests of the shareholders and being their voice in the day-to-day management of the company.

Finally, I will discuss outside groups that have a seat at the deal table including advisors of various types – notably lawyers and investment bankers – and other players including regulators and the press. Even when a company has sophisticated management, and even a professional corporate development staff, advisors are the experts and often have a dramatic impact on how, why and even if a company does a Strategic Transaction. While the regulators and press are not always directly involved in a deal, when they do get involved the impact can be dramatic and their very presence has an impact even if it's just through their inaction.

In each case I'll discuss the role the player has in the deal, the people who tend to fill this role, the economic and incentive model that drives them, and make some general observations about them and how to manage or work with this player.

I hope that this book provides the reader with some insights into the way a deal works and how each of the many players act and why. While this is certainly valuable to deal specialists who do Strategic Transactions for a living, I think it is equally valuable for other business people who may encounter Strategic Transactions on occasion and simply want to understand how they work and who participates. Today, nearly all managers in a company are likely to find themselves, at one point in their career, involved in a Strategic Transaction. Whether they're running a business unit that acquires, or gets acquired, or are brought in to work on due diligence or integration planning, business managers and executives of nearly all sorts are likely to become involved in a Strategic Transaction. When they get involved in such a deal, it is likely to be high profile and risky. It is likely to provide them with an opportunity to shine, or to fail, in a high visibility role that can affect their career. As they walk into a conference room and sit down for their first meeting, it will be invaluable for them to understand the players at the deal table.

2

The Buyers and Sellers and Their People

While most of the companies whose names we recognize today are publicly held, the vast majority of businesses are still privately held and in most cases are owned by either an individual or a family. In the United States alone, there are more than five million small and mid-sized businesses that represent the backbone of the economy.[1] While the highest profile Strategic Transactions take place between large public companies in well publicized, and often argumentative processes, for every such "big deal" there are hundreds of smaller Strategic Transactions taking place every day. In 2002 there were 2,149 reported M&A transactions completed in the United States, though this figure likely understates the number by failing to capture all those smaller deals that were quietly completed between the principals without the help of outside advisors like investment bankers. It is important to note that even of the reported numbers, more than two-thirds were valued at less than $100 million. For every multi-billion dollar deal, there are a myriad of smaller deals that may not make the headlines but are getting done and changing the nature of the companies concerned.

చ్ర ఆక్కు శ

---

[1] In 2000, there were 3,309,000 businesses with 0-4 employees, 1,013,000 businesses with 5 to 9 employees, 606,000 businesses with 10 to 19 employees, and 502,000 with 20 to 99 employees. 122nd Edition of Statistical Abstract of the United States 2002, p 482, (data provided by the US Census Bureau).

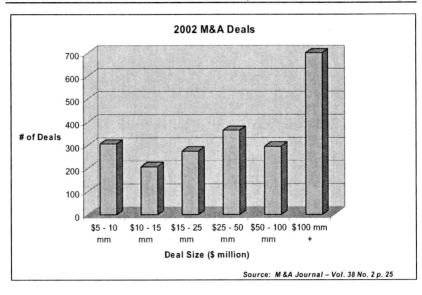

2002 M&A Deals

Source: M &A Journal – Vol. 38 No. 2 p. 25

In today's market, the population of potential sellers includes everyone from multi-billion dollar companies like America Online and Hughes Electronics, to small regional family-owned businesses. While there are certainly differences between a Fortune 500 acquirer and a small family-owned business rolling up smaller competitors, most buyers and sellers share similar goals, incentives. One particularly important lesson to learn is that in the context of Strategic Transactions, bigger does not necessarily mean more complex. It is also important to remember that a bigger deal may have more "zeros" but the smaller a deal is, the more likely even a tiny issue is to become material. In a $2 billion deal, a $50,000 issue like whether the buyer gets to keep the office desks, will never blow things up, but in a $1 million deal, that same $50,000 issue can be a deal breaker. Similarly, while public company deals add the complexity of Securities and Exchange Commission ("SEC") regulations, they are usually done by professional managers who may have far less of an emotional stake in the transaction than a founder of a family-owned business. Thus, as we look at these deals, remember that the players and the complexities they face can be just as interesting and challenging regardless of whether it's a large or small, or public or private, deal.

A. Sellers

1. Summary

The choice to sell is clearly one of the most dramatic, as well as the last, big decision that a company will ever make. It has dramatic and far-reaching effects on everyone associated with the company, both emotional and financial. There are a range of reasons for a company to choose to sell, driven by both internal and external factors. The decision to sell is generally a long-fought and controversial one though it can be triggered and/or accelerated by either an internal decision to initiate a process or an unsolicited offering triggering a decision.

2. The Decision to Sell

From a company point of view there are a variety of reasons to sell. A company may choose to sell because it has maximized its growth in its own market and doesn't think it can expand to new markets – the big fish in a little pond. At this point its best value can be achieved by merging with another player which can leverage its dominance in new markets or with new products. A company may choose to sell because it has reached a plateau and doesn't believe it has the resources to grow any further. An example of this would be a company that has grown in a niche market but now faces the daunting task of competing head-on with a much larger player. A company may simply be taking advantage of what it perceives as a historical peak in its valuation. Some technology companies were wise, or lucky, enough to put themselves on the block in 2000. One could argue that valuations before the "dot com bubble" burst will never again be reached and that selling at that time maximized value for shareholders versus any conceivable strategy for continued growth. In the case of privately-owned companies, a lack of a viable replacement for the founder often drives a sale, as the founder nears retirement. Similarly, smaller companies often become resource constrained from a lack of access to capital. To grow fast some businesses require huge up-front expenditures to buy equipment, real estate or raw material. At some point the opportunities available to a smaller company, even a successful one, may outstrip its borrowing capacity and only a sale to a larger company allows it to take advantage of these opportunities.

There are a myriad of reasons to sell but here are a few examples of why a company might decide it's in the shareholders' best interests to sell.

Peak of Market	Peak of Industry/Sector	New Competitors	Seeking Liquidity Event
Stock Sector is Peaking	*Dominating Niche*	*Getting Noticed by the 800 lb Gorilla*	*Investors Want Return*
Industry sector is peaking and decline is feared	Company is running out of space in a small niche; has picked all the low-hanging fruit	Company has grown its niche to the point where it's attracted big players	Investment has been successful and private investors want to cash out through an IPO or an acquisition
Equity Market is Peaking	*Sector Has Peaked*	*New Competitors Enter The Space*	*Family/Founder-Owned Business*
Stock valuations are perceived to be peaking and decline is feared	Traditional cash cow – strong cash flow in a declining business	New competitors emerge from adjacent geographies, product or customer spaces	Founder is retiring and no heir apparent.

3.   *Economic Model and Their Incentives/Biases for the Seller*

In theory, a company's decision to sell should be driven by the same goals and priorities that drive its daily operation. In the U.S., corporations (both public and private) are primarily driven by the goal of maximizing value for their shareholders. While some courts have embraced the notion that companies can also consider other constituents including employees, customers and the community, it is fairly clear that maximizing shareholder value is the primary, if not sole, goal of a company. However, this is an extremely vague goal and the specific strategy which best achieves it is always a subject of debate. Thus, while in theory a company should always choose to sell when the sale price exceeds the value shareholders will otherwise receive from the continued operation of the company, only one, or sometimes neither, of these values can be measured accurately and certainly. We can never exactly predict the future value of a company but can only guess at it based on projections and forecasts of not only the company's performance, but that of its peers, the industry and the economy as a whole. Estimating the value of an operating company is an art and/or science practiced by everyone from investment bankers to investors to the companies themselves. Since investment bankers are the purported experts, I will discuss the details of these methods a bit more when I discuss the bankers, but suffice it to say that while there are a myriad of models, methods and approaches, there are no certain answers and the most complex model is driven at its base by assumptions which can all be debated. Deciding how much a company is worth or what its prospects are in the future as a stand-alone entity is never exact and usually tainted by the biases and assumptions of those doing the analysis.

Even when a purchase price becomes a certain number, if it is paid in stock or subject to adjustment, its real value remains uncertain. The value of a purchasers stock can move dramatically, effectively lowering the purchase price for a company. One example is VeriSign's purchase of Illuminet. In the fall of 2001, VeriSign purchased Illuminet for a purported purchase price of $1.26 billion.[2] This was a deminimus premium over the market capitalization of Illuminet and was paid in VeriSign stock. On the day of the announcement, September 24th, 2001, VeriSign's stock price closed at $47.01. However, over the next six months, VeriSign's stock price fell to $26.48 and continued to fall. By April 26, 2002 it stood at $9.89. The implied purchase price of Illuminet effectively fell from $1.26 billion to $265 million in a period of seven months. Now while it is possible that had Illuminet stayed public its own stock price would have fallen by the same amount or more[3], it is clear that the price it received did not guarantee its shareholders $1.26 billion but rather simply gave them a chunk of a new set of volatile securities; VeriSign stock. Similarly, a purchase price can be

---

[2] M&A Journal, Vol. 37 No. 2, p. 66.
[3] However, during the same period, the Invesco Telecommunications Fund (ticker: ITHCX) actually appreciated by a small amount.

subject to various contingencies and adjustments related to the post-acquisition performance of the company. A purchase price might have a portion set aside in escrow, only to be paid if the company hit certain sales or customer retention targets. Thus, even the purchase price of the company is rarely a definite value.

The simple mathematical equation of balancing the offer price against the value of the stand-alone company is actually an educated guess at best. As we will see, a variety of biases, preferences and points of view within a company's decision making system will determine how the company values itself and any sale offer it receives. So while a company's decision making may be driven by maximizing shareholder value, smart people within and advising the company will likely disagree on which course of action achieves that goal. This uncertainty helps explain why the decision to sell is usually a complex process with a lot of players. In most companies, the decision to sell is the result of a deep soul-searching strategy process and is usually viewed as a final unappealing conclusion. The very nature of a company and its employees is to be self-perpetuating. Even the most reasonable company management team and board will seek a wide range of ways to maximize value that involve continuing operations and view sale as the "baseline" or worst-case scenario. The decision to sell is usually reached at the end of a fruitless effort to find some, any, alternative that is more attractive and creates more shareholder value. In many cases, it is only considered when an outsider such as a large shareholder or a bidder, forces the issue.

Any decision to sell would obviously have to be approved, and is often initiated, by the board of directors. In almost any situation it would need to be approved by the shareholders. While there are some legal merger structures that might potentially eliminate the need for shareholder approval, it is probably safe to assume that in any real sale of a company or substantially all of its assets, shareholder approval would be needed. For a private company, shareholder approval may be as simple as convening a meeting of the shareholders in a conference room. But in the case of a public company, receiving shareholder approval is a heavily regulated process involving extensive disclosure materials and fairly long time periods.

Closely held private companies, those whose stock is held by a small number of investors, are somewhat different. Technically, any company incorporated in the U.S. has the same obligation to maximize shareholder value. However, in a closely held company with few shareholders that are generally very involved in the operation of the company, the interests of these shareholders will often drive the decision making of the company far more than the simple goals outlined in state corporate law. We will discuss the goals and interests of large shareholders and founders later in the book, but in general terms it is important to note that when the population of shareholders is small and actively involved in the process, you are more likely to see an inclusion of non-financial issues in the process, or the adverse and often competitive financial interests of each shareholder group, come into play.

One exception should be noted which is for the sale of a division, subsidiary or portion of the assets of a company. Since this is a far less material decision, and one that does not mark the end of a company's independent operations, it has far different characteristics. In many cases it will not require a shareholder vote and if it is a sufficiently small portion of the overall business may not even require board approval. The decision making process for the sale of a small portion of a company actually looks a lot like the decision making process for a buyer which will be discussed in the next section. Even if a company is selling a very large part of the business, there is a fundamentally different character to the decision. For the company, it is a strategic decision that is meant to somehow enhance the core business which will continue to operate and this implies that the company still believes that the continued operation of the core business is the best way to maximize value for the shareholders. At an individual level, the sale of a piece of the company has a dramatically different impact. The board and management, with the notable exception of those running the piece which will be sold, will continue in their roles. While some sales trigger a dividend of cash to shareholders (or stock in the acquiring company), more commonly the proceeds of the sale are retained in the companies' coffers for use in growing the remaining core business.

4. *Management of, or Interaction with, the Seller*

A company's decision to sell is like a break in a dam. It triggers a cascade of other events and effects upon the company and its people. The decision is usually hard fought but once made is hard to reverse. Having made the decision to sell, the company becomes embroiled in the formalized process and the inertia of that process will make it fairly unlikely that the company turns away from a sale unless the price eventually offered is exceedingly low. Once a company commits to a sale it changes the very nature of a company. Management and employees are focused on the sale rather than on operations. The board of directors in particular focuses intensely on this huge final decision with which it will be faced. Competitors and customers quickly become aware of the process, the former circling like sharks and the latter quickly questioning the future of their relationship. Once a decision to sell has been made, there is increasing pressure to complete the process quickly to minimize damage to and uncertainty about the company.

It is important to recognize this effect when dealing with a potential selling company. Once you approach a company with a purchase offer, you fundamentally change the nature of the company and the way it behaves. As in theoretical physics, where the very act of observing some subatomic phenomenon changes them, the very act of making a bona fide offer changes the company you are approaching. Similarly, once you make a formal offer, your relationship with the company changes. Pre-offer, a company is much more free to have discussions and, in general, to act. In the status quo a company is free to conduct its business in all, but the most dramatic situations in which it needs to defer to its board of directors or shareholders. However once a sales process begins, the actions of a company are severely limited and will be heavily scrutinized by shareholders and regulators. Pre-offer, a company is likely to be more open to informal discussions and its staff more willing to share information. Post-offer, a company and its staff will clam up as a formal process is organized and then executed under the ever watchful eye of lawyers, investment bankers, regulators, board members and large shareholders. The lesson here is simple: before launching an offer, get as much as you can from the target company since post-offer they are likely to be far more rigid and formal. The same is probably true of other potential bidders. Once a process has begun, while a bidder's actions may not be subject to the same level of corporate governance scrutiny (as will be discussed below) as a seller, they will be much more wary of potential competitors for the target. Pre-offer you are another industry player; but post-offer you are a clear competitor for a particular prize.

B. Buyer

1. Summary

Being a buyer is dramatically different from being a seller. While the decision to sell (unless it is a division or small portion of the assets) is a total and final decision, the decision to buy is one that perpetuates and grows the business. If selling is cashing in your chips, buying is doubling down on your bet. But unless the purchase is of truly dramatic size, it's usually far less material to the buyer than to the seller. A purchase may represent only a small percentage of the overall size of a buyer's business while a sale is by definition one hundred percent of the seller's investment (again unless it is the sale of a division).

The decision to be a buyer used to be a fairly dramatic choice but now is a standard business tool utilized by many, if not most, companies. You can see the use of Strategic Transactions going through several phases over the last few decades. Prior to the 1970s, Strategic Transactions were rarely used and hostile acquisitions were almost unheard of. But starting in the early 1970s, the "art" of M&A began to develop and the hostile transaction became a viable and socially acceptable business tool. Since then both the dollar volume and number of Strategic Transactions has grown dramatically with notable peaks. In the latter half of the 1980s there was an average of 4,000

deals with an average size of $216 million. During the same period in the
1990s, this had grown to an average of 8,600 deals and $1.01 billion.[4]

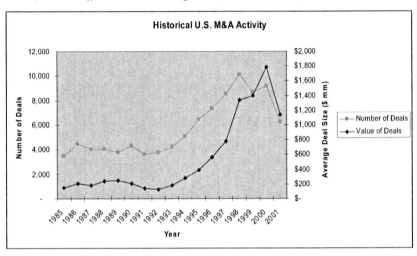

It is clear that Strategic Transactions have begun to have a material impact
on the economic landscape of the U.S., and in recent years Europe and Asia
as well. What is less clear from the raw data is the general shift of Strategic
Transactions from a specialty tool of a few large companies, to a standard
weapon in almost any company's growth arsenal. As recently as the early
1990s, the vast majority of companies – even many of the Fortune 500 –
viewed Strategic Transactions as arcane and complicated deals with which
they were uncomfortable, and depended on more traditional business tools
such as marketing, sales and partnerships to drive high-growth goals. But
today, Strategic Transactions are an accepted and common business tool
employed by thousands of companies. While there are still a few companies
who have a particular veneer as "M&A shops" like Tyco (until its recent
accounting "challenges") and Oracle, there are thousands of companies that
have done one or more acquisition or divestiture, and hundreds that have
been their own in-house teams to support an ongoing Strategic Transactions
effort. This phenomenon will be revisited when we discuss the role of in-

---

[4] M&A Journal Vol. 25, No. 6, p. 36 for 1980s data; M&A Journal Vol. 35, No. 2, p.
25,41 for 1990s.

house corporate development specialists and in-house Strategic Transaction lawyers, in contrast to their outside legal and investment banking counterparts, later in the book.

The result of this shift is that the decision to become a buyer is not nearly as dramatic as it once was. At one time, the decision to become a buyer would have been treated as a dramatic strategic shift requiring long and sustained discussion at the executive and board level and would have attracted the attention and comment of large shareholders. While the board and shareholders will certainly continue to take an interest in any transaction large enough to have a material impact on the company, today, the fact that the deal is a Strategic Transaction rather than a capital investment, marketing plan or regional expansion will not raise eyebrows. Strategic Transactions are just another tool and the question today is not the "how" but the "how much."

Nonetheless, it's important to point out that while Strategic Transactions have become more commonplace, they have not necessarily become less risky. In addition to the legions of professional advisors, there are now hundreds of in-house deal specialists. Over the last three decades all these people have developed a massive collective expertise in doing deals. Even so, Strategic Transactions remain a highly risky way of trying to grow a business or create shareholder value. Various studies suggest that anywhere from one-third to two thirds of the Strategic Transactions done actually destroy value.[5] Therefore, even for a company with extensive experience and

---

[5] Much has been written about the failure of Strategic Transactions. One recent article sites studies that 64% of the M&A deals done in the U.S. between 1985 and 2000 destroyed value. "The Return of the Deal," The Economist, July 10, 2003. Another article argues that when properly measured the number is closer to 30%. Bruner, Robert, "Does M&A Pay? A Survey of Evidence for the Decision-Maker," Journal of Applied Finance; Spring/Summer 2002, Vol 12 Issue 1, p 48. Either reading of the data tells us that Strategic Transactions are no slam dunk and there is a significant risk that a deal will destroy value.

The Economist

seasoned advisors, the decision to do a Strategic Transaction is not taken lightly. But companies have gotten somewhat better at managing the process of the decision and of the deal itself.

For a single acquisition, the decision making process will be no different than for any other large corporate transaction and will probably receive a level of scrutiny commensurate with its size and or profile. In other words, a large, controversial, or politically charged acquisition will receive the same scrutiny as a large, controversial, or politically charged marketing campaign. As with any other corporate decision, there is usually (though not always) a sponsoring business unit which is promoting the idea. This unit will present the idea to an appropriate level of executive management and the decision will be driven upwards towards the CEO or board of directors, as high as it needs to go given its relative importance. For a $10 billion company, a $5 million acquisition may be done with almost no discussion with anyone outside the relevant division. By contrast, the same company doing a $5 billion acquisition would almost certainly seek board approval and in some cases even shareholder approval. But, the level of decision making will generally be based on the size of the individual deal being proposed.

Having said that, given the internal "infrastructure" that a company needs to sustain a formal acquisition program, the decision to use Strategic Transactions as a regular and repeated tool will usually merit a formal decision in and of itself. Each time a company does a Strategic Transaction it will need to field a full team of professionals and go through a series of decision making steps. If the company envisions doing this on a regular basis, it will likely choose to set up formal teams and mechanisms rather than running a repeatedly ad-hoc process. At that point, the company is making a decision not simply to do a single deal, but to become a regular buyer, and that decision does have strategic implications that will have to be discussed. Once a company makes the general decision to use Strategic Transactions as a regular business tool, they will likely give some senior executive general authority. In some cases this is the person's sole job and in others an add-on position, such as "CFO and SVP of corporate development." Depending on how much of the costs the company wants to pull in-house, they may hire a specific purpose team and add lawyers to their legal team with specific skills. While in most companies the corporate development team is a small team of 3-4 "quarterbacks" who pull together resources from other parts of the company to do deals, some companies have built massive deal teams to focus exclusively on Strategic Transactions. In its heyday, the Business Affairs team at AOL had well over 100 staff members - highly paid professionals - dedicated to Strategic Transactions.

Once a company has made the decision to become a buyer, either for a specific deal or for a series of deals as a general tool to grow the business, they will put in place a formal review and decision making process for the deal(s).

There are several reasons why a company chooses to become a buyer. Beyond the decision to acquire a specific target, a company generally chooses to become a regular acquirer when it is facing barriers to growth and/or increase of shareholder value. While growth is usually the goal, sometime a company will be seeking to increase margins or to solidify its market position.

In every case, an acquisition is an alternative to an internal "build" strategy. Every Strategic Transaction is, or should be, prefaced by a "build versus buy" analysis. At its core, an acquisition is an alternative, usually faster, more efficient or more cost effective, method of "building" something that the company wants or needs to fuel overall growth and/or success. As we will discuss shortly, there are many "flavors" of reason for doing a deal. But, in all cases, it is being done as an alternative to "doing it yourself." When a company makes a strategic decision to become a regular buyer it is because it has projected that in many, or most, cases in the future the "buy" option is going to look more attractive than building.

There are a variety of reasons for a company to make an acquisition. A company can acquire a direct competitor to reach a new set of customers or for a brand it has developed. A company can acquire to enter a new geographic region. A company can acquire a target that has developed a product or a technology that the acquirer wants to add to its portfolio. In some cases, a target may even be acquired for the quality of its management or staff alone.

Biotechnology and new international markets are two good examples. Development of new technologies takes time and in some cases no amount of resources will substantially shorten that development time. A company with a powerful sales channel may be willing to pay to acquire companies who have invested that time, since the delay in getting a product to market costs the acquirer more than the premium it will pay to "buy" versus "build." This is particularly true in biotechnology. Given the long development cycle for new drugs, big pharmaceutical companies will often acquire small drug developers once they have gone far enough down the development path with a promising drug. Merck or Pfizer could develop the drug on their own but the lost profits from having to wait an additional five or ten years to start selling far outweigh the acquisition price they pay. Similarly, many companies will use an acquisition to enter new geographic markets, notably outside their home country. Since the process of hiring staff, building facilities and launching operations is far more complicated in a new legal, language and cultural environment, it is often far more efficient to buy a pre-build infrastructure and staff which works in the local environment.

There are a myriad of reasons to acquire but here are some key categories and selected examples of why a company might decide it's in the shareholders' best interests to buy versus build.

Geographical Expansion	Brand	New Products/ Technology	Customer Base	Pure Economies of Scale
Build versus Buy Local Presence	*Repositioning Through New Brand*	*Emerging Technology*	*Bad Product Good Customers*	*Merger of Twins*
Cost of setting up new operations abroad exceeds cost of purchasing local competitor	Much cheaper to reposition company by acquiring existing brand than by trying to remake existing brand	Smaller entrepreneurial companies develop a new technology to the point of effectiveness and a company then acquires them to "leapfrog" the process.	A competitor is not good at providing service or innovating but has a great customer base that is easiest to reach by buying the competitor	Two companies with very similar operations can benefit purely by merging and eliminating redundancies.

2. *Example of the Decision to Buy*

Different buyers have different models for who runs a deal and where the decision making power lies. We can begin by identifying the key players within the buyer. Obviously different companies will have different corporate structures and some will not have all these roles filled, or will have consolidated them into fewer individuals, but broadly speaking here are the key players in the buying decision. At the executive level, the CEO, COO and CFO may all be involved. There may be a head of corporate development reporting to the CFO or CEO, or in some cases reporting to the General Manager of the relevant division. There is the General Manager of the division herself who may also have a divisional CFO or head of strategy. Finally, there will be the in-house attorney who in almost all cases will report to the General Counsel. While other members of management will be involved in the transaction, they will generally have a more peripheral role, providing advice and assistance in execution and due diligence. But it is important to note that these other support functions are also spread across different parts of the organization. One example of a corporate structure could look like this:

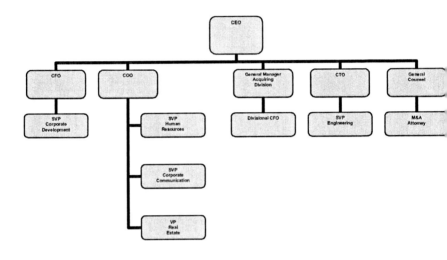

Later in the book we will discuss the major players in the buyer decision making process and focus on each of their particular roles, biases and goals. But, here it is important to note the potential for interplay among them. Every company has both formal and informal power structures and these can often determine how the company makes acquisition decisions. In some companies, the General Managers of the business units have tremendous authority and will drive acquisition decisions in conformance with their divisions' growth strategy, with the corporate staff executives serving primarily to support those deals. In other companies, corporate executive staff may push deals down on divisions, and of course some deals are actually done at the corporate level and don't involve adding to an existing division but rather adding a new division or line of business. Different corporate executives wield different amounts of power in each company. In some companies the General Counsel is a senior decision maker and often has a "consigliore" position to the CEO. In other companies she is a purely legal support mechanism with little impact on business decisions. In some companies Human Resources is a powerful driving factor and company culture is paramount and considered strongly in an acquisition. Again, in other organizations, Human Resources is simply a box that must be checked when doing a deal but never a deciding factor.

Understanding the power structure within a buyer is absolutely key. Since different players in an organization have different priorities, the way you conduct a negotiation is dramatically impacted by who the decision makers are. Even when everyone has the best interests of the company at heart – not always the case – different people have different perceptions of what that is and therefore have different approaches. Lawyers may focus on risk and downside, line managers on product and customers, and executive managers on finance, synergies and market perception. Since most deals are an exercise in exchanging what's of greatest value to me for what's of greatest value to you, understanding the power structure in a company may give you the key to creating an optimal deal. For example, if a buyers' decision is going to be driven by the General Manager who is focused on growing his division, you may be able to extract a higher purchase price (which technically may come out of the corporate balance sheet rather than from his division) if you are willing to tie it to a performance-based earn-out. By contrast, an authoritative General Counsel may nix this approach since earn-out provisions are incredibly complicated and notoriously hard to enforce.

Just as it is important to understand the decision making process to maximize the value of a deal with a buyer, it is also important to understand that process, and the behavior of the buyer for the potential it affords you to protect yourself. For while sellers have the final power to accept or reject an offer, buyers have the power to have a significant, and sometimes irreversible impact on a seller, simply by making an offer, and sometimes making it public. So, it is important to manage buyers carefully.

During the course of a deal, power will often shift repeatedly back and forth between buyer and seller. Here's an example. At the very start a seller can be seen to have power since it determines the timing of launching a sale process, to match the market and its goals. But, if a buyer announces, or even privately makes, an unsolicited offer, some of that power shifts since it is now potentially forcing the sellers' timing. However, if the seller is then able to rebuff the offer, it gains some power because the buyer has now given away information including a "basement price" it is willing to pay. The ability to tell the seller's shareholders about the offer can give the buyer some power since once the seller is perceived to be "in play," its board of directors is burdened with a lot of formal legal obligations. The seller may recapture some power by launching a formal sales process which brings other buyers into the game. But, the initial buyer will regain leverage if it is determined to be the high bidder and enters negotiations. This is just one example of the seesaw effect as power and leverage go back and forth in a deal. Notably, the buyer can exercise a lot of power over, and have a significant impact on the action of, the seller even if it is not the winner or if the seller has not yet chosen to sell. While it is rare that deals become formally hostile and are fought through a full proxy battle, a more subtle form of a hostile approach by the buyer could include approaching members of the board, large shareholders or even the press to bring outside pressure on management to come to the table. Thus, in many ways a buyer is more dangerous before it has even formally become a potential buyer than after it makes an offer.

3. Economic Model and Their Incentives/Biases of the Buyer

Just as there are two layers to a company's decision to buy, there are two layers to the economic model and incentives of the company. In this section I'll discuss these issues for the company as a single entity but in subsequent sections we'll revisit these issues for individual players within a company, and as you'll see the incentives often diverge between a company and its people.

To understand the economic model a company is using to evaluate deals and which drives it to do deals, you have to understand the expectations being placed on it by the market and its shareholders. A company's economic model is driven by a single goal of maximizing shareholder value. The value of shares, and of the company as a whole, is generally driven by a combination of two factors: profitability and growth. Thus the economic model for an acquisition must offer the opportunity for some combination of these two. In theory, a company should be willing to wait a long time for growth or profitability to materialize, if they are large enough. If an acquisition holds the promise of massive growth or profit in five years, this should be a good deal for the company. However, this assumes that investors in the company take a long-term view. When investors are focused on the short term, and flee a stock that doesn't deliver results in the short term (thus dropping the price of the stock), they create an economic incentive for companies to focus on the short term. So even a rational company, driven by the goal of keeping its stock price up, may choose to focus on short-term economic impact. Similarly, if the market has expectations that are biased toward one factor like growth over others such as profitability or the sustainability of financial performance, a company may have an incentive to focus on similar economic metrics in its acquisitions. In a sense, a company may act schizophrenic since the goal of maximizing shareholder value is driven by the stock price which is in turn driven by market behavior. Market behavior is not a singular event but the amalgamation of many investors who have different focuses and different time frames.

This is one way in which private companies may be far more rational in making choices on Strategic Transactions. However, even a private company is subject to the vagaries of the market indirectly since the implied value of the company is tied to the market value of similar companies. The only companies safe from this impact are those private companies where the shareholders plan to continue to own them indefinitely and thus find value purely in the profit generated and growth rate thereof. For any other company – which is the vast majority – maximizing shareholder value is a deceivingly simple economic model under which lies a shifting set of economic goals. On any given day goals can drive companies to seek growth, profitability, protection of capital or even just a reduction in volatility, all in an effort to maximize shareholder value in the form of the stock price, based on the current and sometimes fleeting preferences of the market.

4. Management of, or Interaction with, the Buyer

Any process begins with the initial decision to put a company on the block. Sometimes this decision is made by the seller and sometimes it is thrust upon them. We've already discussed how a seller may decide to sell and how a buyer might force that decision on them. Note that a large shareholder might also force the issue by raising the question of why they aren't being sold or trying to stimulate an unsolicited bid. Once the decision is made or forced, the seller has to decide how they manage the buyer(s) and that means deciding on a process. A process can be as simple as deciding who leads the negotiation or as complex as a tiered auction allowing bids on different portions of the business.

There are several models for managing buyers and the sales process. There is a broad literature which discusses various methods and processes and reviews the pros and cons.[6] Let me briefly review some of the most common models which will help color our discussion of each of the players and the roles they play. The simplest process is a direct negotiation with a single buyer. In this situation the seller directly engages the buyer and as the discussions progress, gives the buyer access to due diligence materials and the parties rough out terms. A more complex process involves simultaneous negotiations with multiple buyers. A variation on this is a formal auction where buyers are contacted and put through a formal bidding procedure. In some cases it will be a two step bidding process where initial bids are received and the population of buyers is culled down to a smaller group that proceed to a second round where they receive more complete due diligence information before putting in a final bid. This is the process Vivendi recently used in the sale of its entertainment properties where Marvin Davis was

---

[6] Excellent sources include: Hunt, Peter, Structuring Mergers & Acquisitions: A Guide to Creating Shareholder Value, (Aspen 2003); Kling, Lou and Nugent-Simon, Eileen

eliminated in the first round and Vivendi then further trimmed the field in a second round. Here is an example of a sales process that is orchestrated in tandem with an IPO process – often an alternative strategy to a sale that a seller may pursue simultaneously:

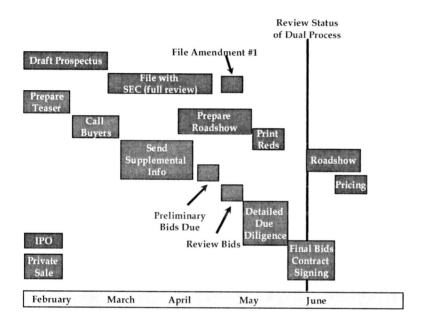

A final variation on the sales process is bankruptcy. This is a situation where management effectively transfers control of the process to the bankruptcy court. Each year tens of thousands of companies file for bankruptcy in the U.S. and while some are liquidated, others are reorganized and maintained as operating businesses under Chapter 11 of the bankruptcy code.[7] There are many reasons a company may choose to go into bankruptcy but once there the board and management have the dubious comfort of ceding

Negotiated Acquisitions of Companies, Subsidiaries and Divisions, (Law Journal Seminars Press 1992); Ginsberg, M.D., Mergers, Acquisitions, and Buyouts, (Aspen 1997).
[7] During the 1990s, there were an average of 56,000 bankruptcy filings each year with a peak of over 71,000 filings in 1991. AmegaGroup.
 www.amegagroup.com/enewsletter/quarterlybankruptcyfilings.htm.

control of the process to a bankruptcy trustee and the bankruptcy court. Bankruptcy sales processes are usually rare although when they occur they can generate dramatic change in very large companies, and impact entire industries. The bankruptcies of both United Airlines and Kmart Corporation are good recent examples of massive U.S. corporations whose bankruptcy and subsequent reorganizations have had impacts on not only their own employees and shareholders but also their whole sector. While some bankruptcy sales simply break down the assets of a defunct company, often the court entertains offers for the sale of the business as an operating entity. This process tends to be even more formal and drawn out than a management-run auction and is open to public scrutiny through published court documents.

Confidentiality is often an important issue, particularly in more complex sales processes. Sometimes sellers will keep the process confidential in an effort to keep buyers from identifying each other. Doing so serves to increase uncertainty among buyers and the fear that competitors may be bidding as well. It also serves to try and block buyers from colluding. On other occasions the seller will choose to publicize a bidding process. The seller may be forced to do this to placate shareholders who want to ensure the process is maximizing value for them. The seller may also do this to ensure that all possible buyers are brought into the process. Buyers will usually press for a confidential process at least early on since if they are public, their very involvement in an auction can bring a sometimes negative reaction from their own shareholder, regulators or competitors.

In the height of the dotcom boom, I was approached by a small company which was conducting an auction process. My company was one of the largest and most obvious bidders for his business and he wanted us to participate. My team had the time to do an initial review and so I was glad to say yes and assign one of my guys to look at the company. But soon after my guy came to me with a problem: the company's lawyer had given him an NDA (non-disclosure agreement) to sign and he carefully reviewed it and noted that it provided one-way confidentiality. We couldn't talk about the auction but the seller was not technically barred from announcing that we were a bidder. This was an unusual term and the young lawyer was being a hard-ass and looking to score points. He had no idea how big a can of worms he had opened. After a long and fruitless argument with him about the unfairness of this term we took a more direct approach. We called the seller's CEO and gave him a clear ultimatum; if the NDA didn't protect our anonymity, we would refuse to participate. He was quick to "correct" his lawyer. But this wasn't an idle threat. As a then $12 billion company bidding on a $50-100 million company, the potential impact of a negatively perceived announcement far outweighed the value of the whole deal. If the press learned we were a bidder and without the opportunity to make a formal announcement and "spin" the deal, shareholders might view it negatively. If those negative views translated into even a tiny 0.50 percent drop in our stock price that would translate into a loss of $60 million of market capitalization – almost the value of the whole deal! For a company with a volatile stock price and where the market is particularly sensitive to news about Strategic Transactions, confidentiality can be a powerful issue for buyers.

We see that when dealing with both buyers and sellers it is important to understand their economic goals and perhaps more importantly their internal processes, and the larger a company is, the more tied it will be to those processes. Even as Strategic Transactions become a more common and understood business tool, different companies maintain substantially different approaches to how they do them and who has what role in the process. Thus far we have considered buyers and sellers as the two players in a deal; now we will broaden the scope substantially.

There is always a tendency to think of corporations (both buyers and sellers) as unified entities. We anthropomorphize them and think of them as individuals, almost as big powerful people. One might say, "General Motors did this" or "Disney won't like that" and personalize companies as if they think and act with a single mind and purpose. When describing or reporting the actions of corporations there is a need to simplify the complexity of the myriad of factors that drive these entities and treat them as a single unit, like a hive or a flock of birds. The press certainly adds to this tendency and it is understandable. It is far easier to report on a company as a single actor, than to tell a complex story of all the shifting and variable players under its skin, so the press treats companies, for the most part, as single-minded individuals. Of course, outside the world of George Orwell and various science fiction movies, they aren't. They are a collection of various types of individuals with differing and often conflicting agendas and interests. This is a particularly crucial insight in Strategic Transactions. Since Strategic Transactions tend to bring about dramatic change and often trigger a fundamental shift in direction, strategy and plans, the differences in these agendas and interests often surface. Thus it is important to look not only at the buyer and seller as players in the process, but also to look "beneath the covers" at the particular players that drive the behavior of these companies. While a small company may have dozens rather than hundreds of thousands of employees, in an acquisition or sale, both small and large companies tend to field a similar group of people who participate in the deal.

The rest of this book is concerned with peeling back the onion and discussing the individual players that work together (both inside and outside) to make these buyers and sellers act. In a way you can think of these companies as those animatronic movie monsters which are in reality operated by a dozen or more different people each with responsibility for a different part or action (the arms, the legs, the fire and smoke from the mouth, etc.). We're now going to look at each of the individuals or groups that together operate "the monster" because understanding their individual roles, biases and motivations is key to understanding the behavior of the companies in which, and for which, they work.

3

The Deal Player Ecosystem

Now that we've discussed the buyer and seller, I'll provide a brief discussion of the broader ecosystem that their interaction spawns. These other players will be the subject of most of the remainder of the book. These players fall into three general categories: internal or company-related players, external advisors and consultants, and independent regulators and press. Together they form an ecosystem that interacts in a variety of complex ways.

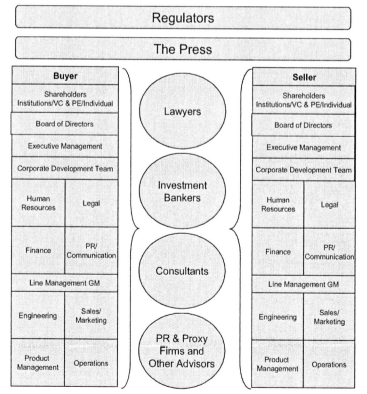

First, we have the internal players within the buyer and seller. If we follow the ownership chain down, each of the companies has a set of shareholders, including large institutions, venture capital and private equity firms and smaller individual shareholders. Below them we find the board of directors and then the executive management team. Reporting to the management team are the line managers that run the major business units of the company as well as various staff functions including the CFO, General Counsel and, in some cases, a head of corporate development and her team. The line manager will have a variety of staff functions reporting to her that may become involved in deals as well, primarily in the strategy development, due diligence and integration planning work.

❧ ✥✥✥ ☙

Second, we have the external advisors and consultants that the companies may hire. Each of the companies may have both their general outside legal counsel as well as specialist lawyers or firms. Investment bankers can be involved in several parts of a deal from advising on the transaction to assisting with financing and, of course, the analyst community that covers both the buyer and seller. Consulting firms are often pivotal in the decision to acquire and the integration planning. There are also a range of other advisors including PR firms and proxy firms (used in a contested public transaction).

Finally, there are the independent players that directly or indirectly represent the public interest. There are a range of regulators that will focus on a deal from the SEC to industry-specific regulators. There is also the press which can be an important factor since the vast majority of employees, customers and shareholders will learn about a deal from them rather than directly from the company.

In many cases, these players have repeated interactions and develop relationships that transcend a transaction. In general, most of the players are involved with the buyer and seller well before the formal decision to do a deal. Outside advisors will woo a potential buyer or seller and provide advice and ideas on a regular basis, in the hope of being retained as an advisor when a deal happens. Similarly, at least the most powerful internal players will be involved in the strategy, planning and decision making process that precedes the launch of any deal. In some cases even regulators and the press are brought in early, to "test the water" for a deal and try to predict and often avoid bad reactions from the public or the regulators.

Even though all the players will likely be brought into the process by the time a deal is launched, there is still often a pecking order as to when they get looped in. As a general matter, an acquisition or sale begins with a decision by executive management, which is usually driven by the strategic goals of the company. In some cases that strategic decision is influenced by work done by consultants; more notably in the case of buyers who have a broad strategic planning process assisted by consultants. The decision often involves early input from the board of directors and work done by investment bankers. There is usually internal analysis done by the corporate development team, often involving senior management of the relevant division. Once an initial decision is made to consider pursuing a transaction, further internal staff is usually added to the process and legal advisors are brought in. At the same time the investment banker role usually moves from an informal and unpaid selling role to a formal paid advisor. Generally, PR firms and other advisors are brought in later in the process as needed. While regulators may be consulted informally in some rare cases, generally they are not involved until a deal is formally announced since in most cases any filings made with regulators are public information. The press is usually involved at the same point.

The timeframe for this process can vary dramatically. In some cases a strategy takes form over a number of years, in other cases over a number of months. In some situations, negotiations take months or even years, particularly with public companies, and in others a deal can be done in days.

4

Executive Management

A. Summary

E xecutive management are the key drivers of Strategic Transactions. They are the players with the combination of the greatest effective power and those most likely to have personal wealth affected by the deal outcome. Strategic Transactions are, by definition, a radical departure from standard operation, from inertia. In the absence of an unusually activist board of directors, it is up to executive management to drive such dramatic changes.

A fundamental tenet of U.S. (and most countries') corporate law is that executive management have a fiduciary duty to the shareholders, as does the board of directors. In a perfect world, the management team's actions would be perfectly in sync with the interests of shareholders. But to the dismay of former law students like myself, we don't live in such a perfect world and there are often conflicts of interest between the goals of management and those of shareholders. Given the unique role and power of executive management, their biases and adverse incentives get amplified in a deal.

In the pantheon of Strategic Transaction decision making, executive management sits on the largest throne. Below them are employees and advisors that must defer to their authority and above them are shareholders and board members who must defer to them because they are focused on the running of the business part-time at best. In some cases employees below executive management will be particularly forceful in advocating for or against a Strategic Transaction but at the end of the day they must defer to their bosses' decisions. While executive management reports to the board and the shareholders, those two groups depend on management for the information that drives their decisions. In the absence of a particularly activist board or large shareholder, management usually drives decisions of the board and shareholders. It remains very rare for management decisions to be overturned by shareholders and even rarer for executive management to be fired by the board. Executive management are unique since they sit at the crossroads of authority and focus. Executive management is therefore the key driver of any Strategic Transaction.

Executive management also have a key role in the effective execution of a Strategic Transaction. They generally drive the broad vision and strategy that plants the seeds of a deal; once a deal is launched they make it happen with a combination of decision making, leadership and sometimes pure force of will. The latter is often a natural result of the character of most senior executives. Executive management tend to be type-A overachievers. They have usually succeeded in most things they've done, have big plans and want/expect high velocity in their careers and their organizations.

In additional to their personal predilection for action, executive management are also the most focused on Strategic Transactions since such transactions will usually have a greater incremental impact on their net worth, careers and personal lives than any other player at the deal table. Strategic Transactions can drive dramatic increases in compensation, career growth and personal satisfaction for executive management in a way that they rarely do for players either below or above them. While there are notable exceptions, as a general matter, executive compensation is at least somewhat correlated to the size of the company that they manage. While the average CEO may take home several million dollars a year, the CEOs of the largest companies take home tens or even hundreds of millions. Perhaps more importantly, executive management are generally not lavishly rewarded for "making the trains run on time." In this age of the celebrity CEO and huge executive compensation packages, executive management is expected to drive dramatic change. By their nature, Strategic Transactions are one of the most rapid and effective ways to drive such dramatic change.

In any Strategic Transaction, executive management of the counterparty is likely to be one of the key forces driving or blocking the transaction. More than any other internal, and most external, players, executive management have powerful and personal direct incentives attached to the outcome of a Strategic Transaction negotiation. One of the keys to success in a Strategic Transaction, both in terms of closing the deal and in getting favorable terms, is managing the executive management of both sides of the deal.

Managing executive management fundamentally means recognizing their goals and crafting a deal that addresses them. Often you can give management what they want without giving away financial value, and you can often bypass negotiating teams and employees by working through channels directly to executive management. This is often the key to success in a transaction far more than synergies, efficiencies or financial structuring. Understanding how executive management thinks can be a powerful tool in getting a deal done.

B.   Executive Management: What's Their Role?

Management is as much about motivation as it is about decision making. Executives make a deal happen by combination of good decisions, leadership and pure force of will. In most companies, executive management's role ebbs and flows during the lifecycle of a deal. But throughout the deal they provide two key things. They are the final decision makers; they sit at the desk where the buck generally stops. While some decisions are made below or above them, the majority of the most important decisions tend to sit with them. As discussed above, this is because employees below them must defer to them and often actively seek to do so. Deferring to executive management is a classic method of C.Y.A. (the crass phrase "cover your ass"). For many mid-level managers, big deal decisions have far more downside than upside and so they're happy to push decisions up to their bosses. At the same time, the board and large shareholders are way too far from the action to have the information necessary to make all but the most general and strategic decisions and tend to defer to executive management, as long as they have some confidence in them. In a sense that's exactly what executive management is paid to do – make the tough decisions.

Executive management also provides leadership. This is a vague term used in far too many "self-help" business books and tends to take on mythic and totally impractical proportions. But here I mean it in the most concrete way. Executive management leads the way. They motivate action both through their position of authority by telling people to do things and through their role as leaders by providing cover and protection for those below them. We can't underestimate the importance of simply telling people to do things. Most organizations, companies, even individuals, are driven by inertia and the status quo. Occasionally a revolutionary is found in an organization that enjoys taking risks and thrives in driving change. But most people in a company focus on their day-to-day jobs. This makes sense since that's what gets them paid. However, when something new needs to be done – like identify acquisition targets, or consolidate businesses – often the organization needs someone to tell people to do it. That's where executive management provides "leadership." By serving as the "buck stops here" guy, executive management also makes mid-level managers safer in making decisions. They effectively "bless" their subordinates' decisions and shift responsibility to themselves.

In the context of a Strategic Transaction, this is particularly important. Such deals involve a tremendous amount of career risk. The decisions in a Strategic Transaction are so large and crucial that screwing up a single major decision can damage a manager's career. Similarly, Strategic Transactions usually drive organizational change that can lead to firings, demotions and other career damage. At the same time Strategic Transactions offer other managers the opportunity to grow and succeed at a higher pace. Executive management is responsible for providing leadership to both spur managers and rein them in, managing both these forces.

Finally, executive management sets direction and "vision." In the day-to-day operations of a company these things are only somewhat relevant. Like a massive ship, the process of turning a company's operations is a very slow and incremental one. But Strategic Transactions are different. They are in a sense each an entirely new start, like a small powerboat launched from the side of the massive ship. Since they can set course in dramatically different directions, they are not subject to the fundamental inertia of a large corporation. As a result, Strategic Transactions are dramatically impacted by the vision set forth by executive management in a way that day-to-day operations are not. Let us take General Motors as an example. Let's assume that executive management at GM made a strategic decision that they wanted to put much greater focus on younger buyers and customers. This vision would eventually be reflected in their current business but over a very long and slow life cycle. The design group might begin to envision vehicle designs aimed at younger buyers and involve marketing and PR in developing that vision. Over the course of four or five years this vision might wend its way into the design of the next generation of cars and trucks launched by GM. But, it would take well over a decade for the vision to be reflected in the full line of GM products, given the life cycle of development and launch for automobiles. By contrast, such a shift in vision would be immediately recognized in the Strategic Transaction team. It could result in a Strategic Transaction within months. For example, it could lead GM to enter the motorcycle market with the acquisition of a major motorcycle manufacturer and, in one fell swoop, substantially change GM's business model with a single transaction. A real-world example of this can be found in the Daimler-Chrysler merger. While Daimler made the strategic decision to broaden its product line to enter the lower price point market, such a shift would have taken a decade if driven through existing operations. Instead, it was quickly accomplished through the merger with a manufacturer already operating in that space. While we may question whether this was the right strategy or maximized shareholder value, it's clear that this vision had a more dramatic immediate impact when implemented through a Strategic Transaction. By the same token, this new vision had a more dramatic and immediate impact on the Strategic Transaction team than it would have if pressed through existing operations.

Thus, in Strategic Transactions, executive management leadership is crucial to set the vision that will determine the nature of the deal, and to drive and sometimes force the decisions necessary to get the deal done.

C. Executive Management: The People and What They Do

All this begs the question: who are these executives that sit at the critical junction in these Strategic Transactions? As is often true, the personal characteristics of these people have a great deal to do with how they reached their positions and how they operate in them. Executive management tend to be type-A overachievers. They have succeeded in everything they've done. They have big plans and want and expect high velocity in their own lives and by extension in the organizations they run.[8] As I mentioned before, in today's environment, CEOs are rarely expected to simply be caretakers of successful businesses, keeping the trains running on time. They are expected to create dramatic change and drive the organizations at high velocity. Velocity can be found in different metrics including growth, financial performance and even product launch. This intensity and high level of focus can be a valuable driver to a deal, but can also become problematic when executives become overly involved in the details of a deal.

It is important to remember the skills and personality traits that are generally found in senior executives, since these traits often drive how they behave. Senior executives generally combine at least a moderate level of intelligence with strong speaking skills and a high level of personal confidence. They also generally have an ability to convey a high level of

---

8 More generally speaking, CEOs have a variety of traits all giving them authority and leadership skills. They are leaders who have the "ability to provide meaning, trust, and values; ability to inspire and energize others to change; ability to listen to others; comfortable sharing information, praise, and resources; people with broad, long term perspectives, convictions about the company's strategic direction, clear managerial philosophy, and the ability to incite the entire company to change for the better." Bennis, Warren and O'Toole, James, "Don't Hire the Wrong CEO," Harvard Business Review, May 1, 2000.

authority and confidence. While some senior executives are brilliant, pure intelligence is not the hallmark of a senior executive. Rather, an ability to influence and motivate people is a more common universal trait. There is a huge literature that delves into the characteristics of a successful executive. Some studies have shown correlations between everything from height, gender, active participation in sports and even lack of baldness, and success as an executive. I won't delve into all of these factors but, as a general matter, it's safe to say that the archetypical senior executive is confident, well spoken, authoritative and at least moderately intelligent. Whether some of these traits are the result of things like height, I'll leave to the sociologists to discover. It is important to note that people with these kinds of traits have a history which may weigh on their decision making. It's good to remind ourselves that most people with this kind of confidence and charisma are accustomed to being respected, promoted and successful. They are not accustomed to being interrupted, ignored or unsuccessful. These preconceptions about the way their lives proceed have an impact on how they approach Strategic Transactions.

One of the results of this set of personality traits and the nature of their role is an inherent pressure to action. Senior executives are expected to drive change and growth, to fix or improve things, and it's in their very nature to do this. They are used to leading people and making bold decisions. As a result, in all situations, there will be a natural aversion to the "do nothing" strategy and a willingness to embrace risk. While there is nothing inherently wrong with acting and embracing risk, a preference to do so may often lead to a suboptimal result, for there are some situations in which doing nothing is for the best. Some companies are not meant to grow but best serve their shareholders running as "cash cows." If I were a shareholder of a buggy-whip company around the turn of the last century, I might well have decided that rather than try to expand into dramatically different lines of business, or do a bunch of creative marketing to try and sustain the buggy-whip as a viable product, it would be best to simply trim staff and run an ever shrinking business at ever shrinking but positive margins, finally selling the assets and shutting down. By her very nature, this approach would be anathema to the CEO of the buggy-whip company.

Senior executives also tend to have healthy egos. This is a virtuous cycle since a strong ego is necessary to succeed as a business leader and such success only enhances one's ego. There are a myriad of stories, particularly in the wake of the dot com bubble, about the excesses of CEO ego. But this is nothing new. It is perhaps a necessary evil that any individual capable of leading a massive organization and fearlessly making decisions affecting billions of dollars and thousands of jobs, must have an inflated ego and sense of themselves, and that making such decisions will only enforce that inflated self. While some executives are wise enough to surround themselves with people who question and challenge them, the fact that the people directly around a senior executive are usually beholden to her for their livelihood, and often already grateful for fortunes made while in their service, there will always be a tendency for an executives inner circle to reinforce the executive's ego and sense of authority. This is an important note since it is something which a counterparty can take advantage of, and which a subordinate involved in a Strategic Transaction must manage.

The combination of executives' "leadership personality," urge toward action and sense of self and ego, can drive them to leave their natural dominion of high level decision making and leadership and cause them to dive into the details. While in theory executive management takes a high level strategic approach, in practice many executives love to "get their hands dirty" and to the dismay of their staff and subordinates may dig into the details of a deal. This is especially true for executives who have an emotional connection to the company or transaction – founders are a good example. Given the excitement and importance of Strategic Transactions, it is quite common for senior executives to wade into the stream of minutiae that make up a deal. In some cases they can add value, particularly when they have experience with such transactions. But in most cases they are too distracted by the range of other issues demanding their attention and instead tend to focus arbitrarily on selected small issues. An executive may dive into a deal only to focus excessively on a particular issue or point that catches their attention but is not particularly material to the overall transaction. One example might be an executive who becomes so engrossed in a particular type of liability that he is taking on that he puts too much emphasis on that point. For example, in some cases employee severance is so important to selling company executives that by taking on this relatively tiny financial liability, a materially lower purchase price can be negotiated. In this situation, even though the adoption of severance liabilities in the abstract is an unattractive and even unreasonable demand, in the context of a lower purchase price or other better terms it may be a good move.

Even more dangerous, an executive may take a moral or personal stance on an issue, again to the detriment of the overall transaction. Some founders become strongly emotionally attached to things like the brand they have built. I have seen selling founders blow up a deal over the issue of the demise of their brand. In these situations, the buyer makes it known that the seller's brand will be wrapped up and their products will be re-branded under the parent brand. This is a fairly common practice particularly with large companies that are trying to manage a huge portfolio of brands and products. The SVP of Marketing at one of my companies was fond of saying "We are a branded house, not a house of brands" and insisted on rolling every acquisition into the central company brand. While in theory this should be of no concern to a seller, a founder may either take offense at the dismissal of his hard-fought and developed brand, or in some cases assume that if no value is attached to his brand that the purchase price must be a "low-ball." This is a good example of an emotional and personal response by a senior executive potentially damaging a deal.

D. Executive Management: Economic Model and Their Incentives/Biases

Management generally gets paid for big wins but is often not penalized for big losses. Bigger is always better, as management is paid based on the size of what they manage and this drives their careers. Similarly, public company executives are paid for short-term dramatic results – the "what have you done for me lately" shareholder reaction. They are focused on shareholder and market reaction. They want to drive their own careers and that means bigger is better and there's a focus on dramatic, and short-term, results. In some cases it also means a focusing on the public relations impact as well. Finally, it may mean pure ego, especially when we're talking about a deal between aggressive competitors.

The management team has an incentive to increase the value of the company and its shares to the extent that they hold stock or options, but they are also interested in keeping their jobs and in enhancing their careers. While in some companies stock and options are not a large component of compensation, they almost always are a major factor for executive management. While this bias exists in all employees, senior management is even more susceptible to the conflict of interest since their compensation and careers are more directly affected by the results of an acquisition or divestiture. For most senior executives in Fortune 500 companies, a moderate increase in the stock price can translate into millions or tens of millions of dollars of value in their options and stock holdings.

Perhaps more concerning is the fact that while management certainly get compensated for successes and rises in the stock price, both through their direct option and stock holdings and through promotion, it is far less clear that they get penalized for drops in the stock price. While their holdings may lose value, they are often given "re-priced" equity to make up for the losses. While some executives are fired or demoted when the stock price tumbles, this if far from a certainty. Again, there is a literature that discusses this so I won't delve deeply, but part of the issue here may be that boards of directors have historically been made up largely of either insiders or people with long-standing relationships to management, and are nominated by management. As a result, they tend to be fairly supportive of the executive management team, and with a few notable exceptions, the large institutional shareholders that would be most capable of challenging executive management tend not to challenge them. The result is that as a general matter, executive management has a strong incentive to drive the stock price up, but faces far fewer penalties when it falls. You can see that the combination of getting paid for big wins and not penalized for big losses will make an executive more attracted to risk. Strategic Transactions are just that kind of risk.

E.   Management of, or Interaction with, Executive Management

Managing executive management means recognizing their goals. Often you can give management what they want without giving away financial value. You can often bypass negotiating teams and employees by communicating through channels, or directly, with executive management.

When negotiating a Strategic Transaction with a company, you will rarely deal directly with executive management unless the company is exceedingly small. Even small founder-run companies typically delegate negotiations or hire an outside advisor. But even though the person sitting across the table may not be the CEO or CFO or Division General Manager (in the case of a very large company), these people are the ultimate decision makers on almost any Strategic Transaction. Influencing them directly or indirectly can be the difference between a good deal, a bad deal and no deal at all.

The first step in managing executive management is to understand their personal goals. Far too often people negotiating with companies, particularly larger companies, forget that those companies boil down to a group of individuals. Even in the case of the largest company in the world – General Electric – it is clear that Jack Welch's views, personality, and preferences played, and still play, a large part in the actions and direction of the company. So whenever dealing with a company, it is important to do as much research and intelligence work as you can on the key decision makers. While they may not be at the deal table, they will most certainly end up in a room with their subordinates reviewing a PowerPoint presentation and making the final "go no-go" decision.

Once you understand executive management's goals you can better craft your approach and offer to maximize your benefits. There are a myriad of variables that may motivate executive management and many of these things are possible to give them without damaging your own interests and position. Often you can trade something worthless to you but valuable to them for something you really want. Several examples are found in the difference between public and private companies. Public company executives are by definition very sensitive to public announcements about their company, projections of their company's financials, and ultimately the stock price as affected by those things. By contrast a private company is usually far less concerned with the first two and doesn't have to worry about the last one. Therefore, in some cases, a private company can craft a deal with a public company that provides the public company with good press, impressive looking numbers and other benefits that it needs. For example, a deal might be crafted to provide the public company with an up-front payment allowing it to hit its quarterly projections, but which also provided the counterparty with a better overall deal. It's important to note here that any deal which affects the financial results of a public company needs to be viewed through the critical eyes of the company's auditors and, in the wake of the recent spate of scandals, will have to pass very careful muster with the auditors. Another example is a strong press push. You can imagine a public company that is being pressed to show a "win" in a particular space and will be willing to cut a particularly good deal to show that "win." For example, imagine that Citibank announced its intentions to increase its focus on services to minorities. In that situation Citibank might be willing to pay a particularly rich premium to acquire a smaller bank that had a strong presence in minority communities to help show that it had achieved this goal. Whether it's a financial, business or public relations goal, you can often structure a deal to give the other company what they want without giving away anything of real value to your side. Often the "thing they want" will be driven by goals of the executive management team.

This leads to a key point about managing executive management. As I've said, in most cases they will not be directly involved in negotiations. In some cases, you may have an opportunity nonetheless to connect with them directly, in effect bypassing the company's chosen negotiating representative (either an outside advisor or employee). This strategy can be powerful, but is also fraught with peril.

On the positive side, the senior executives have the final say on the deal and if you convince them, your work is done. Additionally, senior executives often are less focused on the details of deal terms and rather think about deals strategically. This provides the advantage that they often don't "nickel and dime" as much as professional deal-makers for whom extracting every last bit of value is part-and-parcel with what they do. Thus, if you convince a senior executive that a deal is strategically attractive, they may be willing to cut a far sweeter deal and negotiate far less harshly. But there's a downside to this strategy. Doing an end-run around the formal representative of a counterparty can, to put it bluntly, really piss them off. By going directly to their boss, you've not only taken decision making out of their hands but potentially made them look bad or, perhaps even worse, unnecessary to their superiors. Corporate development and/or investment banking are specialties that tend to suffer from a "anyone can do it" criticism and these professionals can be sensitive to having someone else in their organization cut deals. In the wake of such an end-run you may find that you have made an enemy of the person with whom you have to negotiate and given the level of minutia inevitable in any Strategic Transaction, there will be ample opportunity for them to wreak their vengeance. Thus, if you are considering a direct appeal to senior executives, it is often best to do so surreptitiously or through an indirect connection. Often, a board member, investment banker or advisor, is an excellent tool to get a message to a counterparties senior executives while giving you plausible deniability with your negotiating counterpart.

Finally, in some cases you may find that your counterpart in negotiations is actually a strong ally in managing her own senior executives. Often, the negotiating lead wants to get a deal done but is getting resistance from their own executive management. By offering up relatively immaterial points which you know are important to her executives, you can help your counterpart get the deal done on her side, to both of your benefits.

5

In-House Corporate Development

A. Summary

Now that we've talked about them indirectly, it's time to deal specifically with the deal-maker who is likely to sit across the table from you when you are dealing with a large or medium-sized company. Different people use the terms "business development," "corporate development," and "mergers & acquisitions" to denote a range of different Strategic Transactions. For purposes of this book I'm going to refer to these in-house professionals as corporate development staff, but by this I mean the in-house staff that executes the broad range of different Strategic Transactions. These deal-makers are a relatively recent addition to corporate staffs and take a role that was traditionally held by either outside experts or internal executives who had other primary responsibilities.

The in-house corporate development staff is responsible for some or all of the tasks surrounding Strategic Transactions and works in partnership and in a coordinating role with other parts of the company. They are in the somewhat unique position of managing events where they have little direct control over the majority of people involved. Most of the people involved in the deal are from other parts of the company and report to someone else. They have to work with and manage these people in a project that is generally very high profile and will drive dramatic change through the company. Thus their jobs are inherently highly political and involve a complex network of relationships within their own organizations.

Corporate development staff comes from a variety of different backgrounds including general management, investment banking, law, accounting and even more technical specialties. But as a general rule they are highly aggressive, ambitious, and motivated people who tend to do well under pressure.

While not as directly compensated based on stock price as senior executives, corporate development staff are generally compensated based on a combination of the volume of deals they close, and the success, or perceived success, of those deals. But given the long-term nature of assessing the success of a deal, they are more likely to be compensated based on perceptions about the value or attractiveness of the terms negotiated. This creates an incentive to get deals done, though in some cases metered by the pressure to do good deals. But in all cases the deal itself is their primary task and opportunity to shine.

Since their compensation and overall success are linked to closing deals and to those deals being perceived as successful, managing corporate development staff is strongly linked to driving a deal to close on terms that are perceived as attractive. Managing corporate development staff also involves understanding the internal politics that are so central to their jobs.

B.   Corporate Development Staff: What's Their Role?

While small companies will not have a dedicated "deal guy," most larger companies have started to employ them. This is the result of a fundamental shift that has taken place over the last few decades. Strategic Transactions have only recently become a standard tool of business. Traditionally, companies were grown through organic growth and traditional tools like marketing, sales and some basic partnerships. Strategic Transactions were rare and usually only used by large and sophisticated companies, and a small population of specialist companies like Beatrice and more recently Tyco for whom Strategic Transactions were their bread and butter. But today, most companies view Strategic Transactions as just another standard business tool to help them grow, develop and manage their businesses. In that context, there has emerged a new class of business professionals – the in-house deal-maker or corporate development professional.

Depending on the nature of a company and the expertise of other members of the staff – notably line management – corporate development staff can be responsible for various parts of the deal's life cycle. Let's begin by defining, in general terms, that life cycle: Any deal that has its origins in a general Corporate Strategy that sets out the goals of the company and cases each division or business unit. From that corporate strategy there generally emerges a view as to where Strategic Transactions will be used to achieve goals. One example would be the decision that the company should expand into Europe, which would lead to a choice to either do so organically, or acquire a presence there through a Strategic Transaction such as an acquisition of, or partnering with, a company with a European presence. Once there is a general notion of a goal to be achieved with a Strategic Transaction, you need to develop a Target List. This involves winnowing down the myriad of potential partners/targets/buyers to a short list of those most appropriate to achieve your goal. This analysis includes looking at financial metrics and a wide range of business issues. The company then embarks on Discussion and Negotiation with one or more targets, while concurrently doing Due Diligence on the target and developing an Integration Plan. The Integration Plan's contents will vary based on the type of transaction (partnership versus acquisition versus sale) but will always involve a review of a range of topics including products, technology, financials, customers, human resources, intellectual property and even real estate. There is also the matter of Valuation and Financial Modeling and then eventually Closing. After the deal is closed there is the actual Integration as well. In sum, and of course just as a broad generalization, we might view the key steps of a Strategic Transaction as:

1. Corporate/Division Strategy

A Strategic Transaction is a tool to achieve a goal. You first have to understand your goals before you can identify if a deal is the right tool, and if so, what type of deal should be done. Only then can you find the specific target or company. Whether you're a seller or buyer, the overall strategy of the business must precede the deal used to achieve it. We've already discussed the many reasons why a company might choose to buy or to sell. But in order to reach that decision, the company must first make the choice of a direction. A seller must decide that shareholder value is maximized by a sale; for example, that they can't grow the business further or that competition is about to start encroaching. A buyer must decide that they can't build the relevant capabilities organically and more importantly that those capabilities, products, assets or resources are the right direction to take their business. In some companies, the strategy process is well structured and organized and in others it is non-existent and highly ad hoc. Where there is a separate strategy team, or where line management is adept at developing a strategy, the corporate development team may be relatively uninvolved. In other cases the corporate development team may effectively take on the role of a strategy team, working with line management to help them understand how Strategic Transactions can further their business.

In many ways, this partnering model of having corporate development at least somewhat involved in the strategy discussion will create a far more effective and efficient process down the line. If a corporate development team isn't involved in the strategy process it will be harder for them to prosecute the goals underlying the agreed upon strategy in a Strategic Transaction. By contrast, if they are not at the table, line management and others involved in developing the strategy may not have a deep enough understanding of how Strategic Transactions can be used to help them and may over or under-estimate how they can be used. It is human nature to avoid the things we don't understand and often you will see line managers eschewing Strategic Transactions in favor of the more familiar tools of organic growth that they understand well. Similarly, corporate development staff may overestimate the utility of a Strategic Transaction since they are not comfortable with other growth tools like marketing and product development. As they say, when you have a hammer everything looks like a nail. As a result, a combined strategy effort with involvement by the corporate development team is likely to have the best result both in terms of choosing the right places to use Strategic Transactions and getting them done well.

2. Target List

Once a strategy has been developed, and areas have been identified in which a Strategic Transaction is believed to be the best tool, the next step is to focus on a particular deal. Even more so than the strategy process, this is an area in which it's crucial for corporate development to work hand in hand with line management. They each have a key piece of the puzzle. While line management and their staff understand the characteristics of a partner or target or acquirer that they most need, corporate development understands how to assess other factors like value and financial performance, as well as the very likelihood that the other party will want to buy, sell or partner. Developing the right target list is critical since huge amounts of time can be wasted approaching, or even worse negotiating with, the wrong party.

3. Discussion and Negotiation

This is where corporate development usually takes the lead. First, there must be an initial approach to the counterparty to assess their interest in having a discussion. Sometimes this is done directly by corporate development but often they use an intermediary like an investment banker, a lawyer or a contact in the industry. How you approach a counterparty can set the tone for the negotiation and, therefore, the experience of corporate development in making such an approach is valuable.

Like the beginning of any relationship, establishing dominance, strength and a level of indifference can strengthen your bargaining position with the perception that you are less dependant than the other person on the success of a deal. Once more formal discussions and negotiations start, corporate development usually takes the lead. There are several reasons for this. They have far more experience negotiating these kind of transactions. They are also representing the company as a whole and, as I'll discuss below, line management may have some inherent biases for or against a deal that can color their views. It is also more important to maintain good relations between the two management teams since in most cases they will have to continue to work together. When purchasing a company, you are likely to want, at least for the short term, the management team to stay on and work for you. By contrast, when being purchased, your own management team may be asked to stay on. In the case of a partnership or other non-M&A Strategic Transaction, the two management teams will have to work closely together for the term of the agreement. Thus you usually want to isolate line management from the more belligerent portions of the negotiation. In a sense, you give them plausible deniability to blame corporate development for any particularly harsh stances or aggressive tactics taken during the negotiation. On many occasions, I've had a line manager tell me that she absolutely demands a certain term that ends up enraging the counterparty. But since I've taken the position on behalf of the company, the line manager is free to play a sympathetic role with the counterparty and blame me for the harsh stance. You can even go so far as to structure a position to allow the line manager to "convince" their corporate development team to give in on a point, thus building goodwill with the counterparty.

4. Due Diligence

This is where line management again becomes crucial and there needs to be a strong partnering with corporate development. Corporate development is familiar with the process of due diligence and the more general "corporate level" topics like financial, legal and human resources issues. But on the topics where the rubber meets the road, such as products, brand, technology and customers, line management has the critical level of knowledge and understanding to ensure that you buy what you think you're buying. Corporate development will likely manage the logistics of the due diligence process as well as the formal interaction with the counterparty, including scheduling meetings and trips and requesting material and information. Line management must contribute staff that has the expertise to properly assess this material. This creates a challenge for corporate development since in many organizations the staff contributed by line management may not see the importance of the exercise.

In some organizations, particularly those that do a lot of Strategic Transactions, line management does a good job of communicating to, and motivating, their staff to take the exercise seriously. But in some situations, the staff working on due diligence may view this work as a distraction from their "real job." One way to address this is to plan for the line staff doing due diligence to also be the staff doing integration planning and post-deal integration. Since they know they will be responsible for the business, the deal, or the relationship post-closing, they may take greater care and give greater focus to the due diligence process, because if something is missed, or misunderstood, they'll be the ones cleaning up the eventual mess or explaining away the revenue shortfall.

5. Integration Planning

Failure to do good integration planning is probably the single most common cause of deal failure and disappointment. While bad due diligence can leave landmines undiscovered on occasion, a failure to plan for integration of an acquired company, or execution of a business relationship, can in some cases almost totally destroy the value of a deal. Here again, partnership between the line management and corporate development teams is crucial. Corporate development likely has a standard approach and given their experience should be able to anticipate the key issues and topics that need to be considered. But at the end of the day, it is only the line team that understands the fine points of their operation and, through the due diligence process, the operation of the counterparty. Thus, only the line team can work out the details and predict the specific challenges. For example, the corporate development staff can note that you need to quickly reach out to acquired customers to make sure they don't abandon the relationship, but only the line team will understand how to craft and deliver that message to them. While corporate development may know from experience that staff retention is important, the line team needs to identify who is critical to retain, who they want to retain, and how best to do that in the context of their existing organization.

Integration Planning also serves some related purposes. Since it forces (hopefully) line management to consider the challenges of integration, it hopefully allows them to accurately reflect the costs involved and these have to be factored into the valuation of the deal and the projected financial performance on which the decision to do the deal is based. Failure to take into account both the positive and negative results of integration can lead you to decide to do a deal based on very faulty financial projections. Simply creating a pro-forma by combining two sets of profit & loss statements is not sufficient. On the positive side, there may be synergies to be gained through integration, like the elimination of redundant staff or facilities, and on the negative side, there may be costs to integration like severance or porting customers to a new technology platform. Integration Planning also hopefully forces the line management to think about actual Integration, and assign staff in advance. As I've mentioned, in an ideal world there would be continuity between line staff involved in Due Diligence, Integration Planning and Integration. This ensures that the people assessing the business and planning for post-deal work are the same people who have to live with those assessments and plans. In too many deals, the post-deal Integration team fails to meet the goals of the Integration Plan and simply blames the planners for unrealistic expectations. Thus Integration Planning not only ensures an accurate assessment of the transaction financially, but ensures the most efficient post-deal Integration not only by mapping out a plan but by hopefully bringing in those who will have to execute on the plan early in the process.

6. *Valuation and Financial Modeling*

The other major financial exercise is the modeling of the transaction itself. This involves the analysis of the transaction or targets financials along with the likely changes to those financials as a result of the transaction. These changes could include a variety of "synergies" from the transaction including cost-cutting from redundant expenses and efforts as well as revenue enhancement from the combination of the two entities' resources. The result is a "pro forma" model. I like to describe pro forma with a reference to an old "anti-drug" commercial showing an egg which is then broken into a hot frying pan with the tag line "this is your brain.....this is your brain on drugs." In a sense, this is the financial exercise a company goes through when considering any Strategic Transaction – this is your company's or division's financials.....this is those same financials after you do this deal. It's important to note that the pro forma model is only as good as the data that feeds into it – namely the financial and operational due diligence done on the counterparty and the integration planning and projections. As software developers sometimes say, GIGA – garbage-in-garbage-out, and if the financial projections are weak, so then is the valuation, creating the potential to dramatically overpay for a deal.

7. Internal Process Management

The process for getting approval to do a deal varies dramatically from company to company, and often approval is needed at various stages in a deal, from initial approach to final closing. It also varies dramatically based on the size and importance of the deal. At one extreme there are deals that can basically be approved by perhaps three people, the corporate development manager, the in-house lawyer and the line manager. On the other end of the spectrum, a deal may require approval by a range of people up and down the organization chart of the company including lawyers, various business managers and senior executives up to and in some cases including the board of directors and even the shareholders. Corporate development is responsible for managing and running this process. While they may get assistance, data and material from various sources, they are generally responsible for pulling the material together and coordinating meetings and reviews necessary to get approval. In practical terms this means that the corporate development team spends a lot of time gathering material from people like the member of the due diligence team, outside advisors like investment bankers and lawyers, and corporate staff like the PR and human resources groups, and putting them into formal presentations.

Even just the exercise of scheduling a meeting to review a deal can be a challenge given the seniority of all the people involved.

In larger and more sophisticated companies there may be a very formalized process with which everyone is familiar, and standardized formats for the materials and presentations. In other cases it's a very ad hoc process. In either case it's almost always a significant amount of work and coordination to bring it all together. While this is all internal paperwork, it is essential since Strategic Transactions are generally large enough that they require fairly senior level approval, and risky enough that everyone involved wants to make sure that proper analysis is done and will want to review it in at least summary form.

8. Closing

We will discuss the closing process in more detail when we talk about lawyers. The Closing is mostly a matter of legal documentation. But there are some items that need to be handled by the company's business team, and corporate development almost always owns this responsibility. This might include working with in-house lawyers to gather the appropriate final management approvals and signatures. From press releases and employee communications to setting up funds, transfers and even choosing a location and making sure the right people are in the right places, there may be other staff involved but corporate development are generally there to make sure they get done. Corporate development staff are the final authority on the process of getting the deal done and a surprising number of details tend to come up in getting the deal finally closed.

9. Integration

Post-deal integration is usually owned almost exclusively by the line management team and staff. However, in some cases corporate development will continue to have a role. They will often be involved in monitoring and reporting the financial performance of a deal, particularly in the first twelve months after closing. In cases where the line team doesn't have experience with Integration, corporate development may continue to help them execute on the Integration Plan they helped them develop. In rare cases a corporate development staff member may even be seconded to the line team or even take a permanent role in a newly acquired business. This is often an attractive career track for corporate development staff looking to move into general management. After spending months on a deal, the corporate development staff member may have a deeper knowledge of an acquired business than almost anyone else in the company and this positions her well to make the transition to a management role in the business.

In theory, corporate development staff can provide either leadership or support in each of these efforts. What their role is will depend on the skill sets of the other internal players as well as the politics of the organization. In companies where the line management is experienced with deals, it may take primary responsibility for many of the tasks. In a typical Fortune 500 company, Corporate/Division Strategy and even the Target List will be developed by the relevant business unit. Similarly, the business unit will do most of the Integration Planning, Due Diligence and the actual Integration. In a smaller company or one where the business managers are less experienced with Strategic Transactions, the corporate development staff will either take leadership in these areas or actually do the work themselves. But given the typically small size of a corporate development team and its background, it tends to rely on the business unit staff for specialty expertise that is needed for things like Due Diligence.

Thus, in most situations there is a close partnership between corporate development and the business unit staff. But there are certain tasks that are almost always left to corporate development. They tend to be the experts at Discussion and Negotiation and know how to structure a deal. Similarly they are the ones who understand the metrics of Valuation. In part this is because corporate development is a corporate level staff function. Rather than reporting to any one business unit manager, they tend to report to a corporate executive; typically either the CFO or CEO (or other "C level" executive). In this position, they are tasked with representing the overall interests of the corporation, which are sometimes potentially at odds with those of line management or the staff of a business unit. As we will discuss below, line management often has strong personal incentives for or against a Strategic Transaction. Corporate development staff not only has a role of supporting line management with its specific deal expertise, but also in judging a transaction at the corporate level.

Corporate development staff also has the key role of traffic cop. Beyond the direct work of each of the tasks discussed above, a Strategic Transaction is generally a logistical nightmare. First, there is the ongoing internal decision making process. Given how significant and high profile a Strategic Transaction is, it generally requires approval from a variety of people at various stages. Among the people who may have to weigh in on a deal are senior management, the manager of the relevant business unit, the legal and regulatory staff, human resources and even policy staff. Thus, the pure decision making may require a large number of calls, distribution of material, presentations and meetings. All of this must be coordinated and is generally done according to pre-established procedures, at least in a larger company. Since corporate development staff do these deals regularly, they are experts at managing this process. Similarly, the deal itself has a large logistical burden. In addition to coordinating the efforts of people throughout different parts of the company, the efforts of outside advisors like lawyers and investment bankers must be managed and coordinated. Again the corporate development staff is almost always in charge here. Both of these efforts demonstrate one of the biggest challenges facing corporate development teams. Unlike most other roles in a company, corporate development involves managing projects involving people from a handful or more different organizations within and outside the company. In almost all cases, these are people who do not directly report to corporate development, and in most cases the work they are doing is not their primary job (and often does not weigh heavily on their performance review or result in changes in their compensation). Thus, corporate development staff often finds itself in politically precarious positions balancing different conflicting interests and trying to motivate action in people for whom the work at hand is tangential at best to their careers and compensation.

C. Corporate Development Staff: The People and What They Do

So what kind of people do we find taking on this daunting set of challenges? While they come from a variety of backgrounds with varying levels of direct Strategic Transaction experience, the successful corporate development professional combines several key personality traits and characteristics. Given their leadership role in complex transactions with lots of moving parts, they tend to be very good at coordinating and managing a process. This means they're good at coordinating people, schedules, timelines and tasks. They also tend to be good at dealing with organizational politics. Since they need to manage the varying interests of multiple parties, and motivate people who don't work directly for them, they tend to be good at navigating organizations and working a political structure. In part this may also be how they got their current job. Since corporate development is a very high profile position, it often is an attractive career step and internal candidates tend to be fairly politically connected.

In many companies, corporate development, because of its critical role and visibility to senior management, is also a grooming ground for fast-track young executives. Thus, corporate development staff may be relatively young for their level of seniority and very ambitious. It's not unusual to find that corporate development staff is among the youngest for their title and level within an organization. The same ambition that drives people into corporate development roles may often drive them onwards fairly quickly. This leads to a fundamental split in the way corporate development is viewed in companies. In some companies, this is a staff role that is considered a very specific expertise. In these companies corporate development staff either stays within the group, rising as positions open up, move to highly related roles in finance or under the CFO, or leave the company to gain promotion. In other companies, corporate development is used as a proving ground for high potential young executives. In these companies, corporate development staff is quickly picked off for advancement in line management roles. The most common move is to a planning or finance role within a division with which they have done a lot of work, or to a more general management or CFO role in a business they helped the company to acquire. In either case, it is probably safe to say that the turnover among corporate development staff is usually higher than in other parts of the company.

In terms of specific skill sets, corporate development staff may vary but usually have a combination of competencies. They will have a strong understanding of finance and financial modeling since they almost always have final responsibility for both valuation of a transaction and pro forma financials. They will have at least a basic understanding of their own companies' business and that of the partner/target with which they are negotiating. While they can lean on their business line colleagues for a lot of detail, without a rudimentary understanding of most aspects of the business it will be impossible for them to assess, model and negotiate the transaction. They also need to have strong negotiating skills and the forceful personality that implies. Not only must they be able to negotiate with counterparties, but also to have the authoritative personality necessary to motivate people within their own organization to do their part. Similarly they must be able to manage not only their own small staff but also the outside advisors that are hired. Finally, they must be able to take a broad strategic approach to transactions. While junior corporate development staff focuses on the details of execution, a senior corporate development executive is expected to be able to think strategically and not only execute deals but advise senior management and business unit managers on the strategy of a particular deal and of deals as a general tool.

This leads us to the next question of where companies find people like this for these roles. The answer is that they find them in a variety of places. In many ways, corporate development staff are successful based on certain personalities and skills rather than on strength from a particular background. They are classic generalists that must master a broad range of skills and knowledge bases but are not the experts in most. They must understand finance but are not the finance/accounting staff. They must have a grasp of the business including technology, products, marketing, sales and operations, but not with the level of depth that the people in each of those roles have. They know the basics of legal structures and issues but are not the General Counsel.

Corporate development staff aren't just grown on trees; at least not yet. They come from a variety of specialties. Some are drawn from within the company. Their initial strength will be their understanding of the business itself and the network of existing internal relationships that makes it easier to navigate the organization and get things done. Perhaps even more common are investment bankers. While they'll be discussed in detail below, in general terms they are experts in the financial aspects of executing a deal. They may not have a deep understanding of the business but they understand the details of financial metrics and valuation. Next we have lawyers. In a lot of ways they are the complement to the investment bankers in terms of their deal knowledge. Like the investment bankers they tend to have lots of experience executing deals. But the lawyers are the wordsmiths to the bankers' number crunchers. The lawyers know how to craft an agreement to match business goals and understand the mechanics of actually getting a deal consummated, legally. There are other sources for corporate development staff including accountants and consultants. Accountants understand the financial implications of a deal as recognized by Generally Accepted Accounting Principles. This is important since some of the more arcane rules of accounting can have a dramatic affect on the way a deal impacts the financials of the company. The consultants are the strategists. They will understand the business strategy underlying the deal and be more expert at thinking about the integration of the deal post-closing. I won't go into further detail since each of these specialties will be discussed below. But suffice it to say that corporate development staff are drawn from a variety of places and tend to have and develop broad generalist skill sets.

A final note on the personality of corporate development professionals. Within their organizations, they are the designated deal makers and negotiators. Beyond any natural predilection, they may have to be assertive and aggressive; this is also what is expected of them. While other people in the company are judged by more traditional business performance metrics like sales or customer complaints, corporate development are judged by deals done. One might argue that they should really be judged by their decision making; and that sometimes not doing a deal is the right choice and making it should be rewarded. But at the end of the day, if you don't do any deals, then you don't need any dealmakers. So as a general rule, either formally or informally, a corporate development executive's success is closely tied to closing deals and doing so on terms that are at least perceived to be strong.

D.   Corporate Development Staff: Economic Model and Their Incentives/Biases

This leads us to the economic model that governs corporate development. Here there is a clear problem with judging these staff members based on the financial performance they drive. This is since they play a very temporary role in the deals they do and the businesses they buy. In a perfect world we might keep track of the financial performance of deals done by corporate development and compensate the staff based on that performance. But there are two fundamental problems with this approach. First, it often takes years to see the results of a deal and so it is hard to apply financial performance to real-time compensation decisions. Most large acquisitions take at least a year to be fully integrated, some even longer. During that time, the performance of the deal is still in doubt. But perhaps more importantly, once a deal is done corporate development generally disappears from the process or at the very least takes a distant back seat in the integration process to the line management of the relevant business. Thus it is hard to divorce the performance of the deal from the actions of the managers that take it on post-closing.

As a general matter, corporate development professionals will be compensated and promoted when they're perceived to be driving deals to successful conclusion. Note that there are two parts to this sentence, both necessary – successful and conclusion. A company needs neither someone who drives bad deals nor someone who doesn't close any deals; the former doing damage and the latter just a waste of an office. This may not be the best way to judge performance of corporate development staff but it's often the way it's done. Corporate development staff have other tangential incentives to drive deals to conclusion. First, if they hope to eventually take a staff role their best chance will be in a business that they've acquired. This is since not only will they be among the most knowledgeable about the acquired business and the integration plans, but the acquired business is a unique space in which there is a vacuum of "insider managers" and where the corporate development staffer's knowledge of her own senior management gives her a distinct advantage over the existing management team (clearly not true for the companies' existing internal business units). Secondly, corporate development staff are by definition to some extent "deal junkies." The closing of deals is what excites them in their day-to-day jobs and a series of failed deals, even in the companies' best interests, are inherently unrewarding and unexciting. It's like playing a poker game where the other side always folds; what's the challenge in that?

E. Management of, or Interaction with, Corporate Development Staff

There are several important things to remember about corporate development staff when dealing with them. Each of these lessons can give you an advantage in your negotiations. By contrast, if you are in corporate development or employ such staff, these are good cautionary tales.

Since corporate development staff are deal-makers, there is an inherent bias toward getting a deal done. Getting deals done is how they demonstrate their worth to their organization. As a result, they face constant pressure not to let a deal get away. This is particularly so since they will tend to get line management and executive management excited about a deal and then take the foremost position in executing it. Having created expectations, they will not want those expectations dashed while they are at the helm. But at the same time, they are judged on the basic terms of the deal they cut, most notably the financial terms. As a result, there is an incentive for corporate development staff to sacrifice terms, particularly non-financial terms, to get a deal done, often even when such sacrifices make it a bad deal. One notable example would be legal protections. While the lawyers will push for representations and warranties[9] by the seller, a corporate development manager has an incentive to sacrifice such protections for a higher price or greater certainty of getting the deal. Another example is retention guarantees by existing management. Again while the line manager will press for acquired executives to commit to staying (and tie their stake in the deal price to that promise) because they are concerned with operating the business post-closing, a corporate development manager is incentivized to let acquired management walk away if she can get a lower price on the deal.

By contrast, you may be able to take advantage of natural organizational rifts that are inherent in having a separate corporate development function. Since the corporate development staff are not managing core businesses, they are often less powerful in an organization than line management. Just as you can appeal to executive management to force a deal, you can appeal to line management (as will be discussed below). In either case, the result will be that forces more powerful within the company than corporate development will dictate the pursuit and even major terms of a deal. The point here is that at the end of the day, corporate development is a staff function. While they may have a say in the decision to pursue a deal (this varies from company to company), they rarely have as powerful a say as the

---

[9] For those not familiar with the term, "representations and warranties" are a section of a legal agreement where a party sets out facts that they represent to be true and for which they can be financially penalized if they are false. For example, a seller may represent and warrant that they own their headquarters building free of any mortgage, or that none of their customers has terminated their agreement in the past two years.

division manager who will own the resulting acquisition. But remember that doing an end-run around the corporate development staff can come back to haunt you. As the lead on negotiating and closing the deal, corporate development owns the myriad of smaller issues and decisions that come along with any deal. Here, both executive management and line management will neither understand nor have any interest in learning the issues and will be highly likely to defer to corporate development. But as the adage goes, the devil is in the details and if you have incurred the wrath of the corporate development team (perhaps by going over their heads), revenge can be served in the form of the Chinese water torture of a thousand minor issues, unreasonably raised and debated.

It is also important to note that corporate development staff are repeat players. They will do deal after deal and interact with many of the same counterparties. Corporate development will build ongoing relationships with a variety of players including investment bankers, lawyers, venture capital and private equity firms and even other players in related industries or even in their industry. Thus, unlike the line manager who may have never done a deal before and may never do one again, corporate development staff will be more sensitive to retaining ongoing relationships. They will be more hesitant to abuse a counterparty like a venture capital investor if they think there is a good chance they'll meet at the deal table again. For example, if a private equity or venture firm focuses on companies that are in the same space as the company, corporate development will see them as a regular source for acquisitions. They will seek to balance the goal of negotiating a good deal with the goal of maintaining a good relationship for the next deal. Luckily, those counterparties usually feel the same way.

At the end of the day, corporate development staff are deal professionals and are likely to be the most sophisticated and rational actors in the company when it comes to negotiating and executing a deal. While they may not have as significant a set of biases to try and leverage, they also are less likely to be swayed by such biases. As a result, they will tend to negotiate in a more predictable and methodical way. While they will press hard for good financial deal terms, they will also not let minor points scuttle a deal. On net, they are generally the ally of a deal and usually the easiest people within a company to negotiate with. While you may seek to sway executive management by appealing to their biases, and must likely convince line management that they want the deal, corporate development staff will be your most direct partner in getting a deal done.

6

Line Management

A. Summary

A company is first and foremost the results of its core business operations. Line management run, and grow, day-to-day operations and keep the "trains running on time" and generate the financial results of the company. Line management thus has the most detailed understanding of what the company does, what it does well, and where it needs to go. Line management also understands the market, the competitors, the customers, the technology and the products. Line managers may come from a range of backgrounds but most come up through a career within the operating business. They tend to be focused on product, marketing and/or technology. Their particular focus will usually depend on the nature of the business in which they developed. They tend to have particular strength in managing people and operations, and making things happen at an operational level. While they may not be the most sophisticated (although sometimes they are) and may not have much deal experience (with notable exceptions), they have a deep knowledge of the most core business skills.

More than most staff and executive level managers, line managers' incentives are most directly tied to the "real" or "core" metrics of the business. In practice, their compensation and their success and promotion are tied to the financial and operational performance of the businesses they manage, and as a general matter, managing them involves convincing them that a deal will help them meet those goals. Having said that, it is important to remember that the career of a line manager is also linked to the size of the business she manages, creating an inherent bias toward doing deals. In some cases this incentive is exacerbated by a de-linkage between the capital used in a deal (a corporate asset, cash or stock) and the resulting financial performance (a divisional asset).

ஃ ೞ ஃ

It is important to point out that when I refer to line management in this section, I am subsuming in this category all the line staff that get involved in a deal. While they clearly differ in terms of incentives, expertise and role, for purpose of this book I'm going to assume tight enough management control by the management of a line unit that the incentives and behavior of line staff are at least somewhat coordinated. Clearly when involved in a Strategic Transaction, line management will leverage its staff and resources so, in this context, line management refers to both the leaders of a business unit and the staff they assign to work on the project.

B. Line Management: What's Their Role?

A company is first and foremost the results of its core business operations. While CEOs may be appearing on CNN and the corporate development team is jetting around the world cutting deals, the heart and soul of a company is back at the office, and in the manufacturing plant and at the trade show. Whether it's a technology provider or a tire manufacturer, a company is only as good as its core operations.

Line management runs and grows day-to-day operations and keeps the "trains running on time" and generates the financial results of the company. While it seems obvious, it's surprising how often people forget that line management is responsible for actually running the business. Beyond the maintenance role, line management is responsible for the basic steps that drive strategy and growth. While Strategic Transactions are a powerful tool for growth, those transactions are only effective in building an already strong business. In that sense Strategic Transactions are like an addition built onto a house. If the walls and foundation of the house itself are weak, an addition won't help salvage the structure. Now perhaps a truly massive Strategic Transaction, like a merger of equals, can help fix dramatic problems with a company. But even then, a fundamentally flawed business cannot be saved and it's line management that makes the difference here.

Again it may be obvious but still worth noting that it is these businesses, run by line management, that generate both the cash and the increases in stock price that create the currency for Strategic Transactions. The converse is also true. For a company that is on the selling side of a deal, line management creates the metrics that give the company value and often are themselves (and their retention) an important asset in a deal. Often, an acquiring company is less concerned with retaining the CEO and corporate staff of a target and more concerned with retaining the line management team. Thus, we should never underestimate the importance of line managers' general role and their impact on Strategic Transactions. But beyond that, line managers have much more specific roles in Strategic Transactions.

C. Line Management: The People and What They Do

I won't dwell on the role of line management in the general operation of the business but it's important to note the range of activities for which line management is responsible, because many of these translate to their role in a Strategic Transaction. Among the responsibilities of line manager are managing people, capital expenditures, technology and product manufacturing. They also have responsibility for marketing, sales, business development and all forms of customer relations. They also drive product development and, more broadly, the strategic direction of the business including new products, new services, new customers and new geographies.

Line management understands the market, the competitors, the customers, the technology and the products. Perhaps as key to line managements' contribution is that they have the most detailed understanding of what the company does, what it does well, and where it needs to go. When doing a Strategic Transaction, this is essential knowledge at almost every stage.

Line management's role begins with the strategy process. Any Strategic Transaction starts with the strategic plan of the company and its existing business units and this is driven by line management. Once goals are established, line management is also critical in target identification since they are likely to have a deep knowledge of the other players and the new and developing technologies and products in the sector and related sectors. Line management is also generally involved in negotiations and development of terms themselves. This is true for several reasons. First, line management needs to have input into the way a transaction is done and what is important in a transaction. As an example, when determining what are the key assets and liabilities for purposes of legal representations and warranties, line management are often the best judge. Second, for the management and employees of a target, a relationship with line management and understanding of their plans for the business and employees can be an important negotiating point. Knowing that your future boss plans to keep you and the rest of your management team can powerfully sway a selling executive toward a deal. Finally, since the CEO is going to look to the line management to run the business they will want their sign off on the terms of the deal and so it makes sense to involve them at least passively in the negotiations.

Then we come to the two most important areas of line management involvement: due diligence and integration planning and execution. More than perhaps any other part of a deal, due diligence requires heavy involvement from line management and their staff. While some niche areas like law, intellectual property and labor, may involve specialists, even these areas are dependant on line support. At the end of the day, only line management understands the business well enough to know what's important and what's not. Since due diligence is an exercise in confirming that you're buying what you think you're buying, it's essential to understand which are the really "juicy parts." For example, if a target is being acquired particularly for its strong customer relationships with the plan to substitute the purchasing companies' products, you would put heavy focus on the strength of the customer contracts but relatively little on the intellectual property rights they have over their product design. Similarly, if you're primarily attracted to a targets technology but unimpressed with their management team, you want to thoroughly test the technology and understand any weaknesses, but won't demand strong retention contracts for management. Thus, line management provides not only the resources, but more importantly the knowledge to not just do due diligence, but do it smartly and with the right focus on the critical topics. It is also important that line management is involved since they will have to live with the details of an acquired business. If they aren't involved in due diligence they may end up with problems, challenges and issues that they did not expect nor sign on for.

This leads to the second key area of line management involvement. Since line management will own the process of integrating an acquired business into its own operations, it is crucial that they develop and "own" the integration plan. While corporate development and outside specialists can help guide the development of the plan, it is important that the people who will have to executive the plan have a heavy hand in writing it. Here, the deep operation knowledge is particularly crucial. Successful integration planning has to include a wide range of detailed topics. Technology integration is crucial, including billing, information technology, product development/support and other infrastructure. Integration of marketing, sales, channels and partnership arrangements is also essential. Figuring out how to integrate product lines can also be challenging, and in each of these cases the goal is not just to integrate and remove redundancies but also to recognize the elusive synergies that have likely been part of the basis of doing the deal. Whether this means taking best of breed technology from both organizations, cross selling products effectively to each customer segment, or simply renegotiating advertising deals based on larger consolidated volume, integration planning is more than just bringing things in sync. Integration planning and the execution of the plan often drive the incremental value that makes a Strategic Transaction worth doing, and of course there is the most delicate and challenging integration task – the human component. Line management has to decide who to keep and who to let go. Since they'll be the ones doing the hiring, firing, promoting and demoting, it's crucial they embrace these decisions as their own.

Line managers may come from a range of backgrounds but most come up through a career within the operating business. The traditional route for line managers is to rise up from the ranks of the business, generally from one particular area of specialty. There are significant exceptions to this rule and the trend toward non-traditional paths to line management is growing. Even companies like General Electric which were historically leaders in management development, are starting to move people into fairly senior line management positions from staff functions like corporate development and finance, and the late 1990s created a huge wave of non-traditional line managers as young (often first-time) entrepreneurs found themselves running significant sized businesses and companies. In the wake of the explosion of start-ups, a whole generation of line managers emerged who either had no prior experience or came from non-traditional fields like venture capital, investment banking and accounting. In addition, the technology boom dramatically increased the number of line managers who were pure technologists – the software engineers and technology developers who created the wave of technology products decided to run their own businesses rather that turn that role over to experienced managers. The result is that the traditional line management training track has lost some of its luster or at the very least been presented with viable alternatives.

Nonetheless, the majority of today's line managers are still the product of more traditional career paths within the business unit, and tend to come from a few particular specialties. Perhaps the most common are product development, marketing and/or technology. However, the particular focus will usually depend on the nature of the business in which they developed. Line managers are generally people who have distinguished themselves and who have had a material impact. Moreover, particularly when they are homegrown in the business, they are general those with expertise in what is seen as the core skills and areas of that particular business. As a result, different companies and businesses will mine line managers from different specialties. A dramatic example is found in biotechnology where a medical background, if not an M.D., is almost always essential to a line management career path. Biotech line managers rise up from the ranks of those in the labs. This is a good idea since biotech companies are in large part simply research organizations. The vast majority of value creation in these businesses is in the lab, with sales and marketing generally neither making nor breaking the business. Similarly, in consumer products companies like Procter & Gamble, marketing and sales as well as product development are probably the most likely sources for line management.

But there are certain universal skills that we tend to find in all successful line managers regardless of industry. They tend to have particular strength in managing people and operations, and making things happen at an operational level. This makes sense since at the end of the day people and operations are the conveyer belt down which product and eventually revenue run. In order to make things happen in a line organization you have to get your staff to do it, and to do it in an efficient manner. Now there are some exceptions in the form of business models where staff is so small and highly motivated that people management skills are not essential. A good example is law firms where the rank and file staff are such highly paid and motivated workers that they require an unusually low level of management. However, for the vast majority of business models, effective management of staff and of operations is an essential skill in a line manager. While line managers may not be as visionary or strategic as their corporate staff counterparts (note the use of the word MAY), they are almost universally better at getting the machinery of the business running smoothly.

Thus, as a broad rule, while they may not be the most sophisticated (although sometimes they are) and may not have much deal experience (with notable exceptions), line managers have a deep knowledge of the most fundamental business skills. They are the classic model of businesspeople driving revenue and growth through a myriad of incremental steps; one product, one customer, one sale, one execution at a time.

C. Line Management: Economic Model and Their Incentives/Biases

More than most staff and executive level managers, line managers' incentives are most directly tied to the "real" or "core" metrics of the business. Unlike senior executives and corporate staff, there are very specific and measurable metrics for line management performance. Since they run businesses whose financial metrics are monitored and reported in great detail, they are perhaps most directly tied to their own numbers. The specific metrics will vary based on the type of business and the goals of the company. They can include top line revenue, bottom line profitability or a variety of margin measures, as well as cost metrics. They might also include indirect metrics like number of customers, retention or degradation of customer base, profitability per customer. Which metrics are focused on will depend on the overall goals of the company and its stage of development. For example, an early stage company which is trying to launch itself into a market space may be willing to sacrifice profitability to get a foothold in the market. Here the line manager would be judged by revenues generated and customers captured.

By contrast, in a mature business where little additional growth is expected, a line manager might be judged by her ability to squeeze additional profitability out of a slowly growing revenue base by cost cutting and efficiency. Often, the metrics by which a line manager is judged will depend on external factors like investment banking analysts. If the analyst community focuses on a particular metric, like revenues per customer, there will be pressure on the line manager to focus on this metric as well. Part of the challenge facing a line manager is to ensure that she understands her goals from senior management clearly, so she can manage toward those goals and hit those metrics. This brings up the issue of expectations management. In some well-established industries there may be a stable enough market that performance metrics are understood and expected. For example, in the farming industry there is a fairly well understood set of metrics around how much grain should be produced by an acre of land in a particular region. But in many cases such metrics, particularly as we travel down the P&L from revenue to profit, are hard to predict and subject to a fair amount of volatility. Thus, the line manager faces a political challenge of setting expectations with senior management. She must balance between setting them too low and sending the message that she is not capable of high performance, and setting them unrealistically high, thus ensuring a shortfall. In some cases, how a line manager sets expectations is more important than her actual performance. One line manager with which I worked was particularly adept at setting expectations, and even developing excuses for any shortfalls. The joke was that "he may not hit his numbers, but he doesn't let his numbers hit him."

In practice, line management compensation and their success and promotion are tied not only to the financial and operational performance of the businesses they manage but also to some more intangible variables. Beyond financial performance, senior management often looks to line managers to produce intangible results since, as you recall, they are focused not only on financial performance but also on the stock price (and the correlation between the two is not always perfect). One example is good press and public perception. Biotech companies are particularly focused on these issues. Since biotech involves spending massive amounts of money for a long period before seeing any results, it is important to maintain an ongoing perception that the company's efforts are likely to bear fruit. Thus, line managers may be expected not only to produce eventual financial performance, but also to get enough good press and "word of mouth" to help senior management continue capital-raising to support lab work while awaiting that financial performance to materialize. Similarly, in the entertainment industry, perception and "buzz" often drive financial performance not just in a business unit but across the company. A single product or business unit which produces a hit cutting edge product can affect the entire brand. For instance, if a small unit of Nike that produces headbands can get those headbands worn by major rap stars and create a "buzz," they can enhance the attractiveness of the overall Nike label. Then there are the myriad of other intangibles that line management may be judged on, from workplace diversity to effective hiring and mentoring, to involvement in the community. In one large financial services firm, the manager of a small business unit received particularly strong accolades for his skill in hiring strong talent which they tended to migrate throughout the organization. In another, a manager was recognized for by far the strongest turnout of staff volunteering for a company sponsored charity. These intangible goals will vary from company to company but there are few organizations where line managers are not judged by at least some of these other goals.

As line managers view their careers and goals, there is an inherent conflict between the short term and the long term. In almost any organization there is pressure to produce short-term results. The public markets are driven by quarterly, or more frequent, assessments of company financial performance and these filter down to line manager goals. But by contrast, businesses are often like supertankers, requiring a fairly long lead time to make significant turns and changes. It is rare to find a business where a line manager can make dramatic change happen in a period of weeks or months. More likely the impact of a good manager will be seen over a period of years. As a result, unlike some other corporate staff like corporate development managers where great performance can be seen in short periods, line managers' performance generally takes a bit longer to "ripen." This is not to say that their impact is lesser. In fact, to the contrary, a talented line manager can have a dramatic and fundamental impact on a company's performance over time. The result is that most line managers have a longer time horizon on both their compensation and their careers. Because line management is still the traditional route into more senior line management and eventually executive management, there is a more linear nature to their career track involving the management of ever larger organizations.

This brings me to the issue of size. While a line manager is certainly judged on the impact she has on her business - the incremental change she brings – she is also judged on the raw size of that organization. Certainly in terms of her market value outside the organization, size is a key issue. Size can be measured in financial terms like revenue or in other terms like number of employees or number of facilities managed. But at the end of the day, just as a CEO of a $2 billion company would generally rather be the CEO of a $4 billion company, the General Manager of a $100 million revenue business wants to run a $200 million revenue business. There is also an inherent bias in the way line managers are judged. One might argue that running a small but very high margin business is a sign of success, but most people will associate success with the size of the business run. Thus, line managers will always have a bias toward growth, and even rapid growth. This, of course, is where Strategic Transactions often find a role. Strategic Transactions are a great tool to drive rapid growth in a business in a way that more traditional growth tools like increased marketing and sales cannot. Whether it's an acquisition or a joint venture, Strategic Transactions can allow a line manager to grow her business exponentially in a very short period of time.

D. Management of, or Interaction with, Line Management

In most companies, line managers are the most important initial decision makers for a Strategic Transaction. While senior management may give the final approval, it's line management that guards the gate to beginning a transaction in the first place. Thus, understanding and managing their incentives is critical to getting a deal done. Opposition from a line manager will usually doom a deal before it even begins.

Line managers are excited by deals that help them hit the particular financial metrics on which they are focused. A line manager that is looking for revenue growth will focus on top line performance, while a line manager pressed to produce better margins will be more concerned with synergies driving greater efficiencies and lower overall costs. A Strategic Transaction can also help a line manager meet their non-financial goals. A deal can help build a brand, enter a new space or broaden a customer base. In any case, spinning a deal to point out how it fits with a line manager's goals is key to getting her support.

In general terms though, line managers are likely to be prima facie supportive of Strategic Transactions that help grow their business. All things being equal they will embrace acquisitions and joint ventures that leave them sitting atop a larger, faster growing and/or more profitable organization.

The converse is also true. In the case of divestitures, there is an inherent negative bias by line managers. While a divestiture may be the optimal solution for the company, it leaves a line manager with a smaller organization and generally does not enhance their career. Having said that, there are some exceptions. If a line manager is likely to move with the divested business, her support of the deal will hinge on whether she thinks the buyer provides a better home for her career. In some cases, a line manager running a business that is tangential to the core operations of a company may embrace a sale to a company where her business unit will be more central. One example is found in a deal done in 2000 when UPS sold its truck leasing business to Rollins Truck Leasing, a far smaller company. One might imagine that the managers of the UPS business would actually have been supportive of this transaction. At UPS they ran a business that was clearly not core to the company's operations while at Rollins, their operations became part of the "bread and butter" of the parent company.

Returning to the case of an acquisition or other growth driving transactions, there is an additional bias for some company's line managers. In some cases the incentive to embrace Strategic Transactions is exacerbated by a de-linkage between the capital used in a deal (a corporate asset) and the resulting financial performance (a divisional asset). If a line manager is only judged by the financial performance of her business unit but is not effectively "charged" for the capital used in a Strategic Transaction, she effectively views that capital as "free money." In such a situation, even if the company overpays for an acquisition, if the line manager is only judged by the financial performance of the business in a vacuum, she may still be rewarded for the results of the deal. Thus, in organizations where the metrics used to judge a business unit do not take into account corporate capital put to work on Strategic Transactions, there is an inherent bias towards doing deals.

In the final analysis, the key to dealing with line management is to understand the metrics by which they are judged and their goals for growing their business. It is these things that will drive their support or opposition to a deal, and since line management are the gatekeepers for most initial deal decisions, their support early on is absolutely crucial unless a deal is so large or different that it will effectively create its own new business unit and thus be viewed as a purely corporate transaction.

6

Board of Directors

A. Summary

L ike the executive management team, the board of directors has a fiduciary duty to shareholders. They are supposed to serve as the key and final guardians of the interests of shareholders, notably the multitude of small shareholders, but the amount of independent information they get is fairly limited – executive management is their primary source of data. While board members may be less driven to retain their positions, since for most this is not a primary career driver, they still have some strong interest in remaining on the board. Board members can be employees, senior executives of other companies, or senior leaders of community, social and government organizations. Most board members are nominated to their positions based on relationships with the management team and thus have a certain loyalty to them. This may not be their primary job, but being on a board of directors pays well and is prestigious and so maintaining this role is important to a board member. Another issue which weights heavily on board members is liability. While a board of directors is usually protected by directors & officers (or D&O) insurance, the potential for legal liability above or outside the scope of this insurance, or even just the trauma of going through a litigation, of being sued, is something that board members are very focused on avoiding. Thus, board members have several potentially conflicting incentives including retention of their positions, fiduciary duty to shareholders and the very real danger of liability or at the very least getting embroiled in a legal battle.

B. Board of Directors: What's Their Role?

There is a huge legal literature discussing the role of a board of directors and their legal obligations. Without encroaching too much on this topic I can discuss broadly what their role is in theory and in practice – sadly these two are often substantially different. In theory, the board is the representative of shareholders and has a fiduciary obligation to represent their interests. The board is the final line of defense protecting shareholders who have no direct say in the use of their money, for indeed the assets of the company are bought and paid for directly or indirectly with the money of the shareholders. While some very large shareholders may try to have some voice in the operations of the company (as I will discuss below), they rarely get involved in any but the most dramatic and strategic of decisions. It rests with the board to monitor the actions of management and also to ensure that the performance of the company is accurately reported to shareholders. While there is certainly a gray area, as a general matter any decision which has a material strategic impact on the company is likely to be reviewed with the board of directors. Specific examples of decisions that the board gets involved in include senior executive compensation, larger or more material Strategic Transactions and the broad strategy of the company.

Since board members, with the exception of employee-directors like the CEO or CFO, are only part-time, there are substantial limits to the extent of their involvement. Board members typically spend a number of days each year in board meetings and might spend a number of additional days reviewing documents, reports and material provided by management. But, this is clearly a part-time role and in many cases part-time may mean only an aggregate of a week per year. This inherently limits the level of detail that a Director can absorb. They usually stay at the "10,000 foot level." Perhaps more importantly, they rarely develop primary research by talking to rank and file employees, reviewing product or technology plans or talking to partners or customers. Instead, the vast majority of information that the board uses to make their decisions is provided by senior management. The result is a certain level of circularity in the decision making process.

Executive management requests board approval and then provides them with the data to make the decision on that approval. To quote a recent American Bar Association report, "The ability of outside directors to [oversee the conduct of senior executive officers] effectively, however, has at times been compromised by the practical realities of the relationship between such directors and the senior executive officers – particularly the chief executive officer – of the corporation."[10]

This is not to say that the board are simply a rubber stamp in all cases, but it is important to note that they are not as dramatically independent a review process as one might assume. In some ways they are similar to accountants (which we will discuss later in the book) in the sense that they review information provided by management and make a decision based on that information. Thus, there is a certain level of "GIGO" or "garbage-in-garbage-out."

On the plus side, when management presents the board with accurate and unbiased data, the board can provide significant value. Board members can bring wisdom from experience since they generally are fairly senior and seasoned executives, and the board can bring a broader point of view since they tend to come from other, though related, industries and fields. When functioning properly, a board can help broaden the myopic vision of a senior management team which may have become too laser focused on their existing business, industry, practices and history.

The board also has an important role as a conduit for information to shareholders. One of the challenges of the public company structure is that shareholders are individually too tiny, scattered and numerous to effectively monitor the actions of a company. The board serves as a channel for dissemination of information to the extent that they help ensure that an accurate picture of the company's performance and actions is presented in Securities and Exchange Commission-required publicly filed documents.

---

[10] Report of the American Bar Association Task force on Corporate Responsibility, p 25 (March 31, 2003), www.thecorporatelibrary.com/docs/ABAfinal_report.pdf.

Again, though, their ability to filter is only as good as the information they themselves have. In recent years we've seen the fundamental limitations of this role as many board members of the most notorious corporate failures pleaded ignorance in the face of massive tales of fraud and misrepresentation.[11]

The role of a board, though imperfectly executed in corporate America, is to oversee and monitor the actions of senior management to protect the interests of shareholders, to guide and assist senior management by bringing wisdom and a breadth of experience and expertise, and ensure an accurate and effective communication of the state of the company to shareholders.

C. Board of Directors: The People and What They Do

Being a member of a board of directors is an impressive title and role. Since it is not generally a job in and of itself, most directors have a "day job" though they tend to come from several different backgrounds. First there are Employee directors. In most companies the CEO and perhaps one or two other senior executives are members of the board. The value these directors bring is obvious. As full-time employees and members of the senior management team they provide the board with by far the deepest understanding of the companies' operations and financials. Next there are what I will call the Corporate directors. These directors hold, or are retired from, posts as senior executives of other large companies. In general, they will be well-respected business leaders from companies that are related to the company's activities, though not in direct competition. In many cases the two companies already do business. Common examples are large suppliers, large customers or large partners. Finally, there are what I will refer to as Social directors. These true "outside" directors are generally

---

[11] As the Enron scandal exploded, members of the Enron board of directors went before Congress and asserted that senior management and the auditors of Enron had "deprived them of information they needed to deal with the problems." "Enron directors Plead Ignorance," Associated Press, May 8, 2002.

people with respected roles in the community. They are brought in, particularly with larger high profile companies, to demonstrate both that there are truly independent voices on the board to represent shareholders, and that the company is considering social and community needs in its actions. Examples of such directors might include university presidents, heads of not-for-profit groups and former senior government officials.[12]

There is also pressure for companies to have minority groups represented on their boards though these women or ethnic/racial minorities may come from any of the three groups described. However, given the historical limits on minorities and women in the ranks of senior corporate executives, you are somewhat more likely to find them represented in the third group – executives and leaders from social and community groups. Over time this is beginning to change as women and minorities break through into the executive suites of large corporations in ever increasing numbers.

Being on a board of directors is a threshold event in an executive's career. In most cases, getting nominated to your first board is hard, but after that further nominations are much easier. This stands to reason since that first nomination is like a stamp of approval. Many directors sit on multiple boards in addition to their "day jobs." It comes as no surprise that the time they can spend on their work for a particular company as Director is severely limited.

But if any one set of decisions attracts the attention and efforts of a board it would be Strategic Transactions. In a lot of ways, these events are ideally suited for directors. They involve large strategic decisions that can single-handedly change the nature and course of a business. They generally involve a certain amount of "thinking outside the box" and usually involve some aspect that is new to the business and thus not necessarily within the realm

---

[12] In the mid-90s both General Al Haig and current CIA Director George Tenet joined the board of directors of AOL, and in 2003 former vice president Al Gore joined the board of Apple. Viacom's board includes Joseph Califano, the President of The National Center on Addiction and Substance Abuse at Columbia University. Similar examples can be found in most large public companies.

of knowledge of the management team. More importantly, they are also the kind of decisions where shareholders will look to the board and expect their active involvement.

The board's role in a Strategic Transaction can vary. Different companies have different levels of board involvement and, of course, the size and importance of the deal will also vary the level of board involvement. Generally, a board will get most involved at two key points: strategy and final execution. A board will usually have a role in at least approving the overall strategy of the company and may often be involved in crafting the broad strokes of that strategy. Since this is the underpinning of any decision to pursue a Strategic Transaction, the board will likely have an inkling of the type of deals that are in the pipeline since they've been involved in setting them in motion by defining the overall strategy. Once the board has approved a general strategic direction, they will usually not be formally involved in the interstitial steps of a deal from choosing targets to negotiations. Rather, they will be brought back in near the end of the deal to provide final approval.

There are two notable exceptions. First, it's important to note that in most companies, the board, while not actively involved, will be kept updated on the state of developing Strategic Transactions. This is important since when their approval is requested it is far easier if they have been following the deal as it progresses. Usually board approval is sought quickly and if you have to bring the board up to speed from scratch, it's hard to move quickly. Similarly, while the board may not want to get involved in the "making of the sausages," they do want to have a sense that they are more than just a rubber stamp. Keeping them in the loop as management goes through the process allows them to voice concerns and feel informed. Thus, even when they are not formally involved in a deal process, the board is usually kept updated. Second, there is a substantial exception for the largest Strategic Transactions. While a board will likely approve a deal that represents 1 percent of the revenue of the company with little challenge to the terms, they will feel far differently about a deal representing 50 percent of the revenue of the company. As we've mentioned before, as a deal gets larger the level of focus gets elevated through the organization. As deals get larger the board goes from a more passive rubber stamp to a more active decision maker, and in the case of truly company changing deals, the board may even take primary control of negotiations. Good examples of such deals obviously include the sale of all or a substantial portion of the company but also include acquisitions that represent a significant chunk of the company or even large joint ventures where the strategic direction of the company is shifting.[13]

D. Board of Directors: Economic Model and Their Incentives/Biases

More so than any other player at the deal table, board members have a rich set of non-financial incentives driving their decisions. There are of course financial components. Board members receive an annual salary which though modest by comparison to the pay packages of executives is still significant. More importantly, they get equity in the company which, in the case of some highly successful companies, can end up valued in the tens of millions of dollars.[14]

Beyond money there are other powerful incentives at work for board members. There is certainly prestige and a general advancement of career. Being elected to a board of directors is definitely a sign of success. It also

---

[13] If McDonalds ever decided to shift from its alliance with Coke to an exclusive arrangement with Pepsi, the board would be likely to be involved, and when Chrysler was merged with/acquired by Daimler, the board was heavily involved in the negotiations.

[14] For example, in 2002, board members of Cisco received cash compensation of $32,000 as well as an annual grant of 15,000 options. New directors received an initial grant of 30,000 options. With a strike price just shy of $20, and assuming a growth rate of 15% in the stock price, at the end of 5 years that annual grant would be worth over $300,000 and the initial grant worth over $600,000. Even more dramatic examples can be found in companies that are earlier on the growth curve. For example, in 2000, eBay didn't provide any cash compensation for its directors. But it did grant them 90,000 options in an initial grant and 15,000 each year they served on the board. If a new Director had joined the

provides an incredibly powerful network. You sit on the board with other leaders of industry and in your role as a board member get to meet other business leaders in your work with the company. For example, being elected to the board of directors of Motorola puts you at the table with the CFOs of both Pepsi and Merck. For many senior executives, directorships become a post-retirement job. Boards of directors are littered with "former" and "retired" CEOs.

But in addition to general business contacts and career advancement, there are some more direct benefits to a board seat, particularly for executives who still have their day job. A board seat with a company allows you to solidify a business relationship in a powerful way. If you sit on the board of a major supplier, you guarantee a solid relationship and good terms. Similarly, if you sit on the board of a major customer, you strengthen that cross-company relationship. The converse is also true and many companies seek to strengthen relationships by rewarding the other company's CEO with a board position.

All these powerful incentives create a potential for conflicts of interest with the board members' avowed goal, to serve as the fiduciary for the interests of the shareholders. But there's a powerful counterforce in the form of litigation. Companies almost always get Directors & Officers (D&O) liability insurance to cover people serving on their board of directors. This insurance is supposed to shield directors from shareholder lawsuits, among other things. But the insurance is not a complete shield. First, board members are still open to criminal and securities lawsuits, as the directors of some of the companies accused of massive fraud in recent years have discovered. Even if the insurance covers the financial cost of a lawsuit, it still doesn't shield directors from the arduous and embarrassing process and bad press that comes with it.[15] Especially in the wake of the massive fraud and bankruptcy

---

company in May of 2000 and received 90,000 options, struck at a price of around $55, today those options would be worth over $5 million.
[15] In June of 2003, USAToday ran an article entitled "WorldCom directors' credibility doubted" in which it detailed calls by corporate governance experts for WorldCom board

cases of the last few years, board members have a strong incentive to "cross the t's and dot the i's" when reviewing transactions and financial reporting.

E. Management of, or Interaction with, the Board of Directors

Board members can be powerful allies when trying to get a deal done. They have, of course, strong influence over the decisions of the company, but there are some pitfalls in dealing with them.

Lobbying a board member directly can backfire quite easily. There is the ever-present danger that if you work directly with them you will be perceived as going over the heads of the executive management team, and incurring their wrath. Even more than reaching over corporate development directly to executive management, it is almost impossible to get a deal done, even with the support of a board member, in the face of opposition from executive management. Having said that, getting board support eliminates a key hurdle to a deal and if done without offending management can actually be seen as helping the deal. The key is to sway a board member toward a deal so when the decision hits the boardroom she is supportive.

Board members can also be a great entrée for getting the attention of a company. If you have a relationship with a board member that you don't have with executive management, going through that board member will guarantee you at least a fair hearing. In some ways this is the most powerful way to use a relationship with a board member. It is the ultimate referral into a company and when the email gets forwarded down through the ranks everyone will take it seriously if for no other reason than so the board member can be told it was given due consideration.

In any case, working with a board member has some unique challenges. First you have to remember that this is not (with the exception of Employee

---

members to be ousted from other board positions they held. "WorldCom directors Credibility Doubted," USA Today, June 10, 2003. The article named some of them directly.

directors) her full-time job; this is a sideline. You can't expect directors to have detailed knowledge of operations, financials or strategies. They sit at 10,000 feet looking down on the company. While they can get excited about a general concept for a Strategic Transaction, they shouldn't be expected to dig into the weeds. The details of terms, valuation and integration will be left to staff in all but the most incredibly large deals, and even then, they will be on a steep learning curve supported by staff.

7

Equity Holders

A. Founders

1. *Summary*

We will start with a somewhat unique category of large shareholders, the founders. For many companies, particularly in the technology and biotechnology sectors, founders are still actively involved in the management of the company. For these people, often ultra-wealthy, their interests can go well beyond the basic value of their stock holdings. Often these founders are more concerned with retaining the "culture" they built or with the legacy that they leave behind in the form of this company. These are perhaps the most unpredictable group of shareholders most driven by personal and non-financial incentives. Founders will often resist even financially attractive Strategic Transactions if they would result in the dismemberment, renaming or subordination of their company inside a larger entity. Similarly, they will often push for financially unattractive strategies in order to maintain the culture or character of the company they built.

I encountered one such example in the tail end of the latest technology bubble. My company had made a fairly generous offer to purchase a small technology company with the stated intention of taking their technology and integrating it into our product line. While the major investors and most of the management team was inclined to accept the offer, the founder and CEO could not bring himself to abandon the vision of a large independent company in favor of becoming simply a single sub-product in our catalog.

Only four months after the offer was rejected, the company went into bankruptcy. The CEO clearly recognized the risk, if not the likelihood, that this would happen, but in the face of this as well as a personal financial loss of most of his net worth, he still could not bring himself to make the deal and abandon his greater vision.

→ ℭ℥℧ ←

By contrast, founders can often be a powerful force for more strategic thinking, driving companies away from short-term goals and toward a broader and more strategic vision. Herb Kelleher at Southwest Airlines is a powerful example of this more positive impact of a founder. Eschewing the pressure to grow by adopting the hub-and-spoke strategy of the major carriers, Kelleher insisted on staying true to his model which while moderating growth, drove profitability while avoiding layoffs. The result was a financially successful company with a dramatically more loyal and efficient workforce. During the recent downturn in the airline sector not only did Southwest flourish, but in the greatest form of flattery, it spawned a number of copycat offerings including jetBlue and now Song, the new offering from Delta Airlines.[16]

We find founders to generally have a more dramatic and volatile impact, in one direction or another, than the standard large investor. Not only do they have a huge financial stake in the company, but a sometimes overarching personal stake.

2. Founders: What's Their Role?

Some founders step aside as their business grows and allow a professional management team to take over, but few founders move completely out of the picture. While there are some founders who behave like large institutional investors, being almost completely passive vis-à-vis all but the most massive Strategic Transaction, most take a more activist role in the management of the company and in Strategic Transactions undertaken by

---

[16] Kelleher stepped down as CEO in the summer of 2001 after 30 years, but since then the company has stayed true to the business model on which he built the company.

the company. For the rest of this section we'll set aside the purely passive founder and focus on those that remain involved in the management of the company.

In a sense, you can think of founder as a second title that sits on top of another title. There are founder-CEOs, founder-senior executives, founder-board members and the pure founder-shareholder. In each of these cases they have a primary role that's already been discussed, that of employee or board member. The focus of this section is on the differences that occur when the person is also a founder.

I won't discuss the role of a founder in the early development of a company. There are many texts on entrepreneurship and the launch of new businesses that discuss that role. The issue is what continuing role a founder has after the company has launched. But even in this later stage, it is important to remember the sense of emotional, as well as financial, ownership that most founders feel for their companies, their staff, their culture and even their products.

First of all, the founder is the keeper of the cultural flame. Many, though not all, companies are founded with a core ethos or philosophy or culture beyond simply a product idea. Some people argue that this initial ethos is actually a key to greatness later in the company's life cycle.[17] Even when the founder steps aside for a professional management team, she often has an ongoing role and influence and tries to protect the original culture of the company. However, this role can also turn into a conflict with the new management team who will inevitably want to put its own stamp on the company and its culture. Often this can happen when cultural traits that

---

[17] In his book Good to Great, Jim Collins makes the argument that some of the greatest companies were not founded with a particular product idea but rather with a broad mission statement which formed the basis of their culture. He points, for instance, to Sony, where the company was founded with the goal of helping to rebuild the Japanese economy and turn Japan into a major technology producer. Collins, Jim, Good to Great, (HarperCollins, 2001).

work well in a small company don't translate well to a large one. In other cases it's simply a matter of different approaches.

Founders are also often a symbol of the company and the brand. While some founders shun the spotlight, the classic entrepreneur is a strong personality. It is that strength that allows her to build a business from scratch, in part through sheer force of will. In the process, the founder often gets a veneer of authority and power not only in the company but in the community. Certainly technology company founders like Steve Jobs, Bill Gates and Jeff Bezos continue to bring value to their companies not only through their direct involvement in the business but by mere association. Each of them has become more than just a reflection of the performance of their companies but has a veneer of authority all their own. It's a form of virtuous cycle where the success of the company creates a mystique around the founder which she can then use to the benefit of the company.

Finally, in many cases founders have a core skill in which they continue to excel. A notable example is the more creative skills like marketing and sales as well as new product development. Founders who are visionary in developing new products can continue to provide leadership and insight to the company even if they've outgrown the formal role of a product development manager. The challenge, of course, is to funnel those skills back into the more rigid organization of a larger company.

It is important to note that all of these roles can be viewed from two directions. In large companies that are acquiring, founders will be involved in Strategic Transactions and will add both insight and bias based on their role and history. From the other direction, we can see that founders of companies being acquired in Strategic Transactions also bring insight and bias to the deal.

3.   Founders: The People and What They Do

Again I'll give short shrift to the discussion of the types of people who are generally successful founders. There are a myriad of books discussing the characteristics of the successful entrepreneur. In this context it's good to remember that in order to succeed with a small company, founders tend to be strong-willed, energetic, optimistic people who are able to inspire confidence in both employees and funders. They have some of the qualities of an evangelist in that sense. Founders are not necessarily borne out of prestigious schools and companies, though the late 90s technology boom certainly brought a lot more of that type of person into an entrepreneurial role. Even when they have powerful credentials, it is their personality coupled with a great idea that makes the difference. Some founders bring the great idea with them. They may be technologists, finance wizards or marketing experts. Other founders are simply executing on someone else's idea. In some cases you have one of each type as a founder – the idea person and the execution person.

Once a company has grown, founders often flounder. It's rare to find an entrepreneur who can also operate effectively in a large company, particularly if she is no longer in the driver's seat. They often face a challenge operating in a more structured and rigid organization, but on the positive side, founders who can adapt to a larger corporate structure can bring a combination of a rich industry knowledge and a deep passion for the success of the company driven by a combination of personal and financial incentives.

In the context of a Strategic Transaction, founders may be impediments to the extent that they are willing to eschew a good financial/business deal where they see it as weakening or diluting the culture and vision they've built. By contrast, founders can also be drivers of Strategic Transactions where their vision allows them to see longer term and more abstract benefits of a deal that may elude the more staid and moderate traditional professional managers of a company. Either way, they are likely to voice their views loudly and strongly and hold significant sway over many groups including employees and even shareholders.

4. Founders: Economic Model and Their Incentives/Biases

This brings us to the unusual combination of incentives that hold sway over founders. More than any other player at the deal table, founders have a dramatic set of incentives and biases when it comes to things that have a material effect on the company like Strategic Transactions. This makes a founder a volatile ingredient in any Strategic Transaction.

In most cases, founders still have a massive financial stake in the success of the company. While they have likely been diluted down through the growth (and likely the IPO) of the company, they still may have a materially greater stake than any other individual including the CEO.[18] Strategic Transactions can potentially have a greater effect on the personal wealth of a founder than on that of anyone else with an office in the building.

At the same time, the founder has an emotional and personal stake in the evolution and success of the company. The company is not just a financial investment but an investment of personal capital, heart and reputation. In many cases, the success of the company is the single most important event in the professional life of the founder and the metric by which they are judged. It is far different to found a company and grow it than to be brought in as a professional manager. While Jack Welch certainly developed an emotional bond with General Electric over time, most professional CEOs don't spend nearly that long in a single company and at least in part view themselves as employees. By contrast, founders start out as both owners and operators and even after they have sold off a large part of their stake, they retain that emotional bond and sense of ownership. A good analogy might be between a parent and a teacher. While both have a role in the development of a child, and while at some points the teacher may actually be having a greater impact, a parent will always have a far more passionate link to the child.

Founders have a unique combination of emotional and financial biases and incentives tied to the company. This is made more powerful by the fact that

---

[18] As an example in Yahoo's 2003 proxy statement, years after their initial public offering, founder Jerry Yang still held 6.7% of the common stock, representing over $1 billion in value in the fall of 2003.

as a general matter, founders of successful companies are now independently wealthy. This allows them to be much less concerned by financial results and brings the more emotional and personal biases they have, if not to the forefront, at least into direct competition with their financial goals. A founder who is worth $200 million can afford to see the company turn down a lucrative acquisition offer if he feels it will destroy a beloved culture he has spent years building.

5. Management of, or Interaction with, Founders

In Strategic Transactions founders can play a critical role. They are perhaps the only parties who have a direct emotional stake in the company and are actively involved in its management, and at the same time have a material equity stake and can actually affect a shareholder vote. The traditional public company model has a distinct separation between equity and management, and as we discussed, part of the role of the board of directors is to bridge that gap. In founders we often find people sitting on both sides of that equation. As a result, a founder's views on a Strategic Transaction often have to be taken into account since even if she is no longer in a senior executive position, she may still have the power to block the deal from happening.

As I've said before, it is always dangerous to go "over someone's head." It is perhaps even more dangerous when it comes to founders. In many cases their formal title does not reflect the level of informal authority they have within an organization, and the professional management team and even the board are often threatened by this. If you are perceived as having appealed to a founder and tried to leverage that authority, you may get a powerful negative backlash. At the same time, founders can be an excellent informal sounding board for potential Strategic Transactions. Even when they are no longer actively involved in management they retain perhaps the best "network" within all levels of the organization. A founder may be able to give you guidance on everything from whether the shareholders, board and CEO will entertain an offer, to whether the rank and file employees will react well and can be retained.

In some cases, particularly where most of their net worth is still tied up in company stock, founders will have personal financial goals that will make a Strategic Transaction attractive or unattractive. As an example, a founder who has most of his net worth in the company and is looking to retire may be eager to have the company sold if it will cause him to recognize a liquidity event. If he is no longer going to be actively involved in management he may prefer to be able to shift his wealth to a more diversified portfolio and it may be hard (or he may even be barred by contract) to sell a large stake quickly where a Strategic Transaction might offer him the opportunity to take out cash. However, when dealing with founders it is important to keep in mind their non-financial goals as well as the more obvious financial goals. Founders will often have a heightened sensitivity to maintaining the culture they created, protecting the employees they hired and even just retaining the personal image of someone who built a successful company. By crafting a deal that meets these goals, you can often drive a Strategic Transaction to a successful conclusion without sacrificing anything material. You may be able to get support from a founder with relatively low cost commitments to retain staff, or even something as simple as retaining the brand or logo.

The key with founders is to understand their personal preferences and "hot buttons" and try to find a way of making them happy without sacrificing something of value to you. Since financial considerations are often secondary to them, this may be easier than it would be with an arms length investor for whom price is the bottom line, and often the only line.

B. Public and Institutional Shareholders

1. Summary

Public corporations are usually owned by a large population of relatively small stakeholders who each own tiny percentages of the stock and take only a mild interest in the day-to-day affairs of the company. These shareholders are focused entirely on the market value of their holdings, and to a large extent they depend on a combination of the board of directors, the regulators like the Securities and Exchange Commission (the "SEC") and the bigger shareholders, to actively protect their interests. It is this population of relatively unempowered small shareholders that the SEC, and the securities laws which it enforces, were in fact created to protect. There are the occasional activist small shareholders who might show up at a company's annual meeting and ask challenging, or sometimes even annoying, questions, but for every one of these, there are tens of thousands who are entirely passive. Even the most basic level of shareholder involvement, the annual proxy vote on major issues, is usually met with apathy. Response rates, particularly from individual shareholders, remain low even for substantive issues.[19] Of course the fundamental challenge here is an adverse incentives problem akin to the challenge of voter turnout in elections. Since each small shareholder realizes their incremental impact on the company is deminimus, they have no individual incentive to participate. They rely on the other shareholders, and regulators, to protect their interests. Therefore, management of a public company will usually focus on the small number of large shareholders who take an active interest in the activities of the company, as well as the regulators like the SEC, who in effect act as a proxy for the large population of apathetic small shareholders.

---

[19] For example, in 2002, the Conseco proxy vote which included election of directors and approval of a new executive compensation plan received votes (either for or against) from less than 60% of all shares outstanding. Even for such an important and controversial issue as studying the sale of the company, in 2002 the average percentage of shares outstanding voted on the issue was only 77%. Annual Corporate Governance Review - 2002, (Georgeson Shareholder Services, 2002), p 11, 15, www.georgeson.com/pdf/02wrapup.pdf. Even these numbers substantially overstate the number of shareholders actively voting since under Rule 452 of the New York Stock Exchange, the "ten-day rule," brokers are empowered to vote shares held in street name when shareholders fail to vote them ten days before the deadline. "To give an idea of the impact of the broker vote, consider this - ADP reports that for the "street name" accounts covered by its programs, the average response rate for annual meetings during the 2002 proxy season was 89%. Actual shares returned accounted for 66%, with the remainder of the shares generated by routine ['ten day rule"] broker votes." The CorporateCounsel.net, quoting David Drake, managing director of Georgeson Shareholder, www.thecorporatecounsel.net/E-minders/archive/Jan2003.htm.

The larger shareholders, usually mutual and pension funds and occasionally a very wealthy individual, may be somewhat more activist but even they have limited time to devote to delving into the activities of a big company.[20] A mutual or pension fund typically holds stakes in hundreds of companies and is constantly reviewing potential additions and subtractions to the portfolio[21] and such a fund usually has a relatively small staff. The result is that these funds can devote very few man hours per year to the review of a particular company's operations.

However, some large shareholders may have other interests beyond the movement of the stock price. A large shareholder may seek to influence or even control the actions of the company and in that case, while they may have a long-term goal of increasing the value of their stock holdings, they may have other short-term goals like buying up a larger stake or getting a seat on the board of directors. This is a good demonstration of the potential for shifting and conflicting interests, even among shareholders. A large shareholder seeking to increase her stake in a company will actually want the price of the stock to go down, at least in the short term, to allow her to accumulate it cheaply. She may even want it to go down in order to ferment discontent among shareholders to allow her to gain a board seat or even control of the company.

2. Public and Institutional Shareholders: What's Their Role?

In general terms, the role of an institutional investor is to gather funds from a large number of parties, directly or indirectly, and invest them in a coordinated manner seeking to maximize returns within the context of the investing goals and approach, if any, by which they have been restricted.

---

[20] According to one study, even the most activist mutual funds spend only 0.005% on governance effort, in contrast to 0.5%-1.0% on management of investments. Black, Bernard, Shareholder Activism and Corporate Governance in the United States,, papers.ssrn.com/sol3/delivery.cfm/9712036.pdf?abstractid=45100, citing Del Guerco and Hawkins The Motivation and Impact of Pension Fund Activism, Working Paper, (University of Oregon and Lundquist College of Business).
[21] As of June 30, 2003, the Fidelity Magellan fund has shares in 222 different holdings. The Fidelity Contrafund has shares in 536 different holdings.
Source: personal.fidelity.com/products/funds/mfl_frame.shtml?316184100.

This group includes mutual funds, pension funds, insurance companies and a variety of other institutions holding large pools of cash.

While large institutional investors don't have any legal fiduciary obligations, they are often the only active voices of the shareholder base. To be clear, their fiduciary obligations are solely to maximize the value of their own funds holdings for their fund investors. But in some cases this goal coincides with protecting the interests of the broad investor base of a company. However, there is a constant conflict in most funds between two goals, maximizing the value of their stakes in companies and remaining a passive purely financial investor.

It is important to note here that I am only talking about large institutional and mutual funds like CalPERS (the California public employee pension fund) and Fidelity (the largest mutual fund complex). In a later section I will talk about venture capital and private equity investors that affirmatively seek to take an active role in management of the companies in which they invest and often have board seats with those companies. But for traditional institutional investors there is a strong interest in remaining totally passive when it comes to corporate management. There are a variety of reasons for this stance including the notion that they are pure stock investors who aren't beholden to other shareholders and retain the flexibility to buy and sell shares solely for the benefit of their own portfolio value. They also are very sensitive to the danger of becoming embroiled in the management issues of the company and potentially opening themselves up to legal liability for having effective control.

3.   Public and Institutional Shareholders: The People and What They Do

Managers of institutional investors are paid for performance. I won't go into tremendous detail here since this is not a particularly core player at the deal table and lots has been written about fund managers. In short, they are paid when their funds outperform alternative investments. Since anyone can simply put their money into an index fund, the goal of every fund manager is to provide a return far enough in excess of the index or otherwise distinguish themselves sufficiently to justify the cost of their operation and salary.

However, some would argue that there's an imbalance in the way this compensation is meted out. Arguments have been made that fund managers are over-rewarded for high performance and under-punished for low performance. For example, many argue that during the technology bubble of the late 1990s, many fund managers over-invested in speculative technology stocks to drive up their performance in many cases in contravention of the investment guidelines they were supposed to be operating under. One could also argue that fund managers are punished for "visible blunders" more than for others. In other words, a fund manager will be punished more for investing in a highly visible failed company than is justified by the performance of his fund. For example, even if a fund has good performance over the past few years, if it had a significant investment in Enron or WorldCom or Imclone the fund manager may be subject to greater criticism than if she had invested in less controversial stocks. All this is to say that while fund managers are judged by what, on its face, is a highly objective financial measurement, there are certain non-financial or pseudo-financial issues that can impact perceptions of their performance.

Fund managers can come from different backgrounds but they're far more homogeneous than some other players we've discussed. They tend to have strong finance skills and when the fund is sector-focused they may have a sector background. They either grew up in the fund environment straight out of college or business school, or usually came over to the "buy side" from "sell side" positions like investment banking, sales & trading desks of major financial firms, or research analyst positions. They generally have traditional finance and accounting educations with some specialist exceptions.[22]

---

[22] For example, many biotechnology fund managers may actually be MDs (medical doctors) since the sector requires such a strong understanding of medicine.

These finance types spend their days researching companies, making buy/sell decisions and monitoring their portfolios and the market. Even the most well staffed fund has a small number of bodies to cover hundreds of companies. They monitor not only the companies they own but also ones they are considering owning, and even though they get lavish support from the trading desks that want to execute their trades and the research analysts that want their votes on industry rankings, they are still stretched pretty thin. The result is that they only focus on a company when (a) they have a substantial investment and (b) something dramatic is going on, and remember that in the context of these funds, a substantial investment is usually measured in hundreds of millions.

4. Public and Institutional Shareholders: Economic Model and Their Incentives/Biases

Institutional investors, and by extension their staff, are paid to provide the best possible financial returns while executing investments based on a sometimes vague, and other times laser sharp, investing approach. These approaches can be as clear as investing in mid-cap technology companies and as vague as investing in growth stocks. But within the context of the investment approach, their goal is to maximize returns (and of course inherent in this is the flip side of avoiding losses which are basically negative returns).

While institutional investors are focused on maximizing the financial return on their investments, they often find themselves in a position to effect a company's strategy by virtue of their large shareholding. Funds have such a massive amount of money to invest that it is difficult for them to avoid ending up with material stakes in companies. There are many examples of institutional investors holding up to 5 percent or more of a large public company. This is particularly true of the most massive funds that are constantly challenged to place material amounts of money in each investment.[23] While this may not give them any kind of legal control, in the context of a highly splintered shareholder base where a large percentage of the shares don't get voted, their stake may actually allow them to sway decisions and certainly gets the attention of management. They also get the attention of management for a more basic reason -- fund stakes are so large that a decision to sell can actually affect the stock price and move the market. This puts the fund and company management in an odd financial embrace. The company wants to keep the fund happy just to ensure they don't sell a large stake and push the price down by doing so, and the fund is, in some cases, bound to the company since they can't effectively sell their stake without depressing the value of it and thus reducing the value of the holding (i.e. after selling the first 1 percent the price begins to decline and the remaining 4 percent gets priced at lower and lower levels).[24]

The result of this inherent conflict is that while institutional investors assiduously try to avoid getting involved in company operational issues, in extreme cases where they see management materially damaging the company and thus the value of the stock, their fiduciary duty coupled with an inability to easily divest their stake forces them to become more activist. The question is where that threshold is met, and the answer varies from investor to investor. Additionally, in the wake of the spate of recent accounting frauds and other irregularities, many institutional investors have begun to feel that a more general activism, beyond specific "triage cases," may be necessary. In a sense, there is the potential for a waking giant scenario where the institutional investors start to become more involved in

---

[23] A good example of this is the Fidelity Magellan Fund, which at the time of writing was the largest mutual fund with assets in excess of $65 billion. Consider that in order to make an investment representing 0.1% of the funds assets Magellan managers need to place $65 million. Since there are a limited number of massive companies, as you shift down the scale to mid-sized companies at the bottom of the Fortune 500, this becomes a material percentage of ownership. For example, at the time of writing, Growth Fund of America owned more than 5% and Capital Guardian Trust (a subsidiary of Pacific Life) owned more than 10% of Sprint PCS.

[24] Someone familiar with Wall Street trading practices will probably note here that there are a lot of mechanisms for funds to dump their holdings in such a way as to mask their identity and moderate the effect on the stock price. The best example is the use of other firms to execute the trades is smaller chunks. While this reduces the impact of a massive sale, large funds are unlikely to totally avoid impacting the stock price if they dump, even over time and through other parties, a large amount of stock into the market.

issues of corporate management. Since they have the critical mass of a large stake and the ability to focus some attention on a specific company, they could actually do so. Having said that, they have remained very hesitant to do so in the past and it is more likely that they will wait to see the impact of regulator efforts like Sarbanes-Oxley and focus their wrath on only the most dramatically mismanaged companies.

5. Management of, or Interaction with, Public and Institutional Shareholders

Institutional investors aren't involved in all, or even most, Strategic Transactions. In fact, all parties concerned, including the institutional investors themselves, will usually try to avoid involving them. However, in situations where a Strategic Transaction can have a dramatic impact on the value of the stock, or in situations where the stock has tumbled and there is a perception that a radical change is needed, institutional investors may feel a need to get involved. Beyond an outright sale or a merger of equals, even an acquisition can fit into this category if it's either big enough or dramatic enough in terms of changing the strategy or business model of the company. In that situation, institutional investors may make their voices heard.

For some transactions a shareholder vote is required and if the success of the vote is in doubt, active lobbying of the institutional investors will be a key to success. It is dangerous for an outside party to lobby an institutional investor. Since they rarely get involved in a Strategic Transaction they will often simply refuse to voice an opinion. Even where an institutional investor voices an opinion, it is only relevant to the extent that either (a) there is going to be a shareholder vote or (b) they hold enough stock to have sway over management. In either case, they have only an indirect impact on the decision of management, and the downside is that an approach to an institutional investor will clearly be seen by both management and the board of directors as an end-run around them.

Approaching an institutional shareholder as an entrée to instigate a discussion with management or the board is also not necessarily effective. If the institutional investor has a particularly close relationship with the CEO or a member of the board it may be an effective channel, but usually there are better channels in the form of lawyers and investment bankers. Furthermore, the CEO or board may still take offense at communication with their shareholder, since if they decide not to pursue the deal they now need to provide an explanation to the shareholder. If you are already in friendly discussions with a company, theoretically, you might lobby institutional shareholders, but even then most CEOs and boards would want to limit such contact. In rare cases with very activist institutional shareholders there might be meetings to explain and discuss potential deals, but in the age of Sarbanes-Oxley you have to be particularly careful about such one-on-one communications of what may be non-public information.

There are also legal issues around lobbying shareholders directly, particularly if the party lobbying is also a shareholder or is planning to make a material offer for a controlling interest, or total acquisition, of the company. Before making such an approach, it is worthwhile to consult legal counsel. This brings us to the situation where formal lobbying of shareholders is allowed but heavily regulated. In a friendly deal, the counterparty approaches shareholders hand in hand with management, or more accurately, management and the board approach shareholders with a proposed transaction with the counterparty. However, if management and the board rebuff an offer, the counterparty does have the option of making what is called a "hostile" approach. This is both a term of art and usually an accurate description of the mood among the parties. In a hostile deal, the counterparty in effect goes over the heads of management and the board and appeals directly to shareholders, telling them that their representatives (the board) and employees (management) are not serving them well. Again I will defer a detailed discussion since there is a rich literature that discusses hostile M&A transactions but, in short, the counterparty will try and cause a shareholder vote to be initiated and then try to convince shareholders to elect her representatives to the board, at which point the new board would approve the transaction. Now in this relatively rare situation, institutional shareholders can often be the absolute lynchpin and each side will aggressively lobby them for their support.[25]

There are some rare occasions where institutional investors themselves will initiate communication on a Strategic Transaction. While they often call the investor relations team of the company to ask questions and get information, they usually do not try to directly influence management decisions. However, in situations where they feel strongly enough about a deal (where they think it can have a material impact negative or positive on the value of the company) they may feel a need to step in. In those situations they will generally communicate with executive management and it's pretty unlikely that they would take it onto themselves to communicate with the counterparty.

At the end of the day, it is fairly rare for either party in a Strategic Transaction to approach institutional shareholders directly over a deal. In situations where institutional investors will actually be concerned, a message about the deal, and its value, is usually delivered indirectly through communications with Wall Street analysts or public press statements. Paraphrasing the hit man in the film *Grosse Pointe Blank* about his victims, "If I come to visit you there's probably a good reason....you probably did something to deserve it." The same might be said about an institutional investor getting involved in a company's Strategic Transaction.

C. Private Investors

1. Summary

In this section I will refer to angels and venture capital firms which are associated with early stage start-up companies and private equity firms

---

[25] But it is a very rare situation indeed. It is safe to say that a hostile deal has a far far lower likelihood of succeeding and will take dramatically longer to close if it does. It is fair to expect that if a deal turns hostile, you should expect it to cost millions of dollars more (if not tens of millions) in legal and other advisory fees and take months longer.

which are associated with larger established private companies or spun-off divisions of public companies, or the leveraged buyout (LBO) and/or management buyout (MBO) of public companies, together as private investors. Among venture capital investors there are a variety of sub-types that invest at different stages of a company's development. For the sake of simplicity I will generalize here to two different types: angels and venture capitalists. By angels I am referring to wealthy individuals, as well as "friends & family," that are usually the first source of start-up funding when a business is just an idea on paper. By venture capitalists I am referring to professional investors who will tend to invest after angels when a little more meat has been put on the bones of an idea in terms of developing product, testing market and establishing relationships with partners and sales channels. While a venture capital firm will usually invest in a business that is barely up and running, or in some cases hasn't even really launched, entrepreneurs usually start with angels with whom they have a personal relationship and who have a higher level of trust and are willing to fund them with just a concept in hand. During the height of the technology boom in the late 1990s, it was not unusual for an entrepreneur, particularly one with a solid track record, to get funded purely on the basis of a power-point presentation of her idea or business plan. In recent years venture capital firms have gotten back to more traditional investing patterns depending on either the entrepreneur herself, or the angel investors, to bring a business concept at least to the point of having a prototype or "beta test" level of product before investing.

While there is a core similarity in the roles venture capital and private equity firms play, there are some important differences. They both provide money, expertise and a network, but while venture capital firms need to get deeply involved in the basics of operating and growing the nascent business, private equity firms can leave those basic issues of blocking and tackling to the more experienced and established management structure and focus more on complex financing issues and Strategic Transactions. In a sense, if an investment is successful, a venture capital firm evolves its role into something much like that of the private equity firm. In both venture capital and private equity firms, the staff can come from a number of different sources beyond homegrown talent. Some staff are recruited straight out of undergraduate or graduate school and trained up (this is particularly true in larger established firms), but staff are also recruited from the professional finance fields, the ranks of entrepreneurs and from industry itself. Together they provide a mix of expertise in the industry sector they're focusing on, finance and banking and the growth of a new business. In all cases they tend to be highly motivated, bright, and excited about growing new businesses, and their economic model is heavily tied to the success of their invested businesses, with the vast majority of their long-term compensation coming in the form of equity in their portfolio businesses. The result is that their incentives are closely tied to the success of their portfolio and particularly to the liquidity events that turn their equity in the portfolio companies back into cash.

The key to working with private investors is to understand the status of their portfolio and thus their need to recognize gains and the timing of that need. As long as you understand the private investors' key incentives, they can be a valuable source of expertise and a powerful network of relationships that can be leveraged.

2. Private Investors: What's Their Role?

While there are substantial differences between angels and venture capital firms on the one hand and private equity firms on the other, and even within those two categories there are a broad range of variations on the basic model, you can view them all as having a similar overall role. They provide capital, expertise and a network of relationships.

Money is the first and most obvious thing that private investors provide to a company. In the case of start-ups, they need this capital to create their business and in later stages to grow it more rapidly once the business model has been proven. In the case of public leveraged buyouts the management team may think the company is undervalued in the public markets and wants to take it private by buying out the public shareholders, with the presumption that in a few years they can either take it public again or sell it to an acquirer, at a much higher value. In any case, the need for money is the key and first motivator driving a company's management to work with private investors, and these firms have it to give. Over the last two decades the amount of money committed to venture investments has risen dramatically. While in the wake of the technology boom there's been a precipitous decline in capital commitments, it's clear that in the long term venture capital will be a much more significant source of liquidity for smaller companies than it was in decades past. Even in the post-dot com bubble era, the "run-rate" for venture capital investments is an order of magnitude higher than it was in the mid-1980s. Similarly, there has been a substantial rise in the venture funding done by large corporations, and while some recent scandals over revenue recognition with regard to those deals has put a damper on such corporate venture investments, in the long term the amount of venture investing done by corporations has clearly moved to a much higher level.

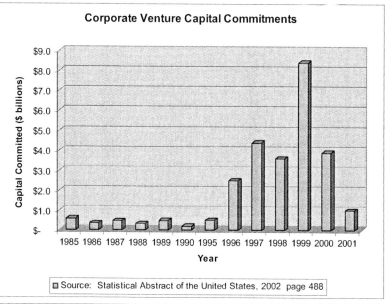

Corporate Venture Capital Commitments

Source: Statistical Abstract of the United States, 2002 page 488

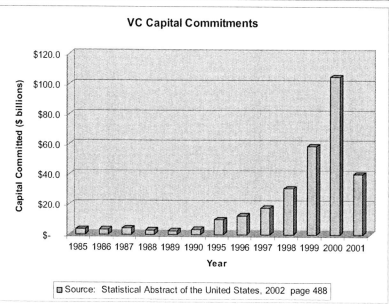

VC Capital Commitments

Source: Statistical Abstract of the United States, 2002 page 488

Unlike traditional private investors, corporate venture investors typically have dual goals. They are certainly looking for a financial return. But in addition they are usually seeking to fulfill corporate strategic goals like those of a corporate acquirer. Examples of typical corporate goals could include preferential relationships with the smaller company for use of their products, or access to the smaller company's customers or technology. This is where some of the controversies have arisen, when investing companies were accused of generating "round-trip revenue." In these deals the corporate investor would make an equity investment in a smaller company with an unwritten quid pro quo that the smaller company would use some or all of the investment dollars to purchase the bigger company's product, or the bigger company would take payment for its services in the form of the smaller company's stock. This provided the smaller company with a cash infusion, or effectively free services/product, and a powerful equity relationship. The larger company was able to turn balance sheet cash into income statement revenue. However, in many cases this revenue has been deemed fraudulent and companies have been forced to restate their financials to remove it.[26] One of the highest profile examples of this is found in AOL Time Warner. During the height of the technology boom, AOL took payment for advertising in the stock of several small start-ups and accounted for these payments in stock as revenue. These and other "barter transactions" are now the subject of various SEC investigations and are one

---

[26] "The [SEC] staff discussed situations in which two (often simultaneous) transactions occur between two parties. For example, a vendor could provide goods and services to a customer for cash and at the same time purchase an equity interest in the customer for cash. In such a situation, the staff would look through the exchange of cash and view the transaction essentially as a non-monetary exchange (i.e., goods and services for equity investment in customer) governed by Accounting Principles board Opinion No. 29, Accounting for Non-monetary Transactions. The vendor would typically record (a) the investment at the value of the shares received or the goods sold (whichever is more readily determinable), (b) the net cash outlay or receipt, and (c) revenue equal to the value of the investment plus or minus any net cash received or paid. However, the SEC staff cautioned that it is important to understand the substance of the transaction and that in certain situations such "revenue recognition" may be inappropriate. For example, if the customer does not need the goods or services or buys quantities that exceed its needs, the transaction would appear to lack substance. In such situations, the appropriate accounting would depend on the underlying substance of the transaction." Financial Reporting 2003, (BDO Seidman LLP, 2003), p6-7.also found at www.bdo.com/about/publications/assurance.

of the factors that have driven substantial financial restatements that buffeted AOL's stock price in the last few years.[27]

So while corporate venture investors are certainly going to be more cautious about such cross relationships, there are enough other benefits to close relationships with smaller start-ups, including a "beachhead" towards an eventual investment, that corporate venture investing is likely to continue at robust levels.

It is also important to note that money is a self-fulfilling prophecy. Without being insulting, private investors are sometimes like cattle. They tend to follow each other into investments. There's a good and efficient reason for this. A lot of due diligence goes into an investing decision. Whether it's an early stage business or a public company going private, the investor needs to delve deeply into the financials, examine the product, review the management team and strategy, and a myriad of other things. When one reputable investor has done that and decided to invest, it gives other investors the comfort to do a somewhat more rudimentary job of due diligence. Since these firms generally have small staff trying to place massive amounts of money, it helps to be able to sometimes shortcut the arduous process of investigating a deal. Therefore, not only does a "lead investor" bring their own money but they smooth the way for other investors to put in money as well, relying at least in part on the work they did.

Beyond money there are other, vaguer but nonetheless important, things that private investors provide to their portfolio companies. They can provide critical expertise in areas that the entrepreneur or seasoned manager may not have experience. In the case of entrepreneurs, the angels and venture capital firms can provide expertise in all the basics of setting up and launching a business. While some entrepreneurs may be experienced at building a business, often they are specialists who have developed a great

---

[27] "SEC looks at AOL Time Warner," USA TODAY, July 24, 2002; "AOL to Restate Troubled Unit's Revenue Again, Vexing Wall St.,," New York Times, Section C , Page 1 , Column 5, October 24, 2002.

new product, technology or approach. While a technologist, doctor or scientist may know how to develop something new and valuable she may have no idea how to turn it into a product, test the market, and structure and negotiate deals with the myriad of outside entities she needs to work with, including manufacturers, suppliers, sales partners and even regulators. Angels and venture capitalists can provide her with this expertise. Even a more established entrepreneur may not have some of the key skills to grow a business from a small private venture to something larger and more marketable, either to a potential acquirer or to the IPO market. Here angels and venture capitalists can provide the crucial difference between a company that stays small and one that burgeons into a major corporation over time. They can help the entrepreneur structure the organization for growth including putting in place systems for hiring and managing larger numbers of people, building a sales channel, creating the right legal structures and, often critical and ignored, building a good financial reporting and accounting system. As part of this exercise, the angels and venture capitalists can help find the talent to make these things happen. It's not unusual for a venture capital to actually insert one of their staff into a portfolio company as the CFO or COO, and in other cases to take one of their stable of "entrepreneurs in residence" and actually insert them as the new CEO, shifting the founder to a more appropriate product-focused role like CTO. The larger companies in which private equity firms invest don't need this kind of basic help, but they may still need other expertise. The executives of even a medium-sized public company may not have a deep understanding of complex finance or the planning and execution of Strategic Transactions. A private equity firm may be able to help them structure the financing to do an LBO/MBO and post-privatization, help them plan for an eventual liquidity event in the form of an IPO or sale. However, it's important to note that even experienced private investors have limitations in their skills and insights, and often the hubris of having large amounts of capital can cause them to push their opinions beyond the range of their skill. This is when a management team must walk a careful balance between not angering their key investors and turning away from bad ideas generated by those investors.

Private investors also provide a unique access to a network, both in the form of their other portfolio companies and through their well-connected staff. Private investors tend to focus on one or a number of sectors, and thus, they end up invested in a portfolio of related companies. They try to foster cross relationships between these companies, encouraging them to cross market, use each other's products and share technologies. In a lot of ways, these portfolio groups look a lot like the traditional Japanese Keiretsu or the Korean Chaebol and I'm sure that private investors look at those structures as models. While the relationships that bind the companies in a private investor portfolio are looser than in these Asian corporate networks, in part because control is not as centralized and in part because there may be stronger anti-competition regulation in the U.S., they still tend to benefit the individual member companies. Beyond the portfolio network, a private investor offers a company the relationships of their staff. Senior partners in large private investor firms tend to be very well connected and through their investment in the company actually have a very direct financial stake in its success. Thus, they will often help these companies get connected with large customers, partners and eventually sometimes with acquirers. Again, however, the management team must guard against a natural bias by private investors. They will have to decide when the relationships that the private investor wants to foster are the best choices for their company, and in some cases may spark a conflict with the private investor by choosing an alternative partner that is not part of the private investor's network.

In most cases the private investor, particularly if she has a substantial stake and was the lead investor in a round of financing, will have a seat on the board. However, her level of involvement will vary dramatically based on the nature and maturity of the company. Private equity investors tend to allow the management team a fairly free hand in running the company since these tend to be well established and mature companies with seasoned managers. By contrast, angels and venture capitalists may become very involved with the day-to-day operations of their portfolio companies. Beyond sitting on the board, an investor in an early stage company will do a lot of "hand-holding" and have input, sometimes firm input, in most of the bigger decisions. One of the interesting dynamics in a private investor-portfolio company relationship is the slow decline, sometimes forced, of the investor's influence as the company matures. While this is sometimes a natural separation with the venture capital firm pleased to be able to focus on other portfolio companies and the company management excited to stand on its own two feet, in other cases there is animosity or open conflict as the management team asserts itself and the venture capital tries to stay involved. In a lot of ways, you can view the venture capital-portfolio company relationship like that of a parent and child, with the middle stage looking a lot like the teen years. Maybe by contrast, the private equity firm's relationship with its portfolio company looks more like that of a parent and a child going off to college. But, as my parents would be quick to remind us, the return to these private investors may not be as emotionally rewarding but is usually dramatically more financially rich than for a parent. When was the last time you heard of a child handing her parent a check at graduation for ten times the cost of tuition?

3. *Private Investors: The People and What They Do*

Private investor firms tend to be relatively small teams of highly credentialed experts. At the first tier you will have founding partners who may have provided part of the funding or simply had a network of relationships to get the fund going. They then hire a small staff of professionals and generally a very limited number of support staff. They tend to remain lean even as they grow. For example, one private equity firm with over $5 billion under management which has been the lead investor in several $1 billion-plus transactions has a global staff of only 22 professionals and a handful of support staff. The professional staff of these firms come from a variety of specialties, and provides a balanced mixture of several key skills. Some staff are "homegrown" and recruited directly out of undergraduate and graduate business programs. This became more common in the last decade with the influx of funding to these firms that caused them to have to grow their staff at a more rapid pace, but traditionally, most of the staff of these firms comes "pre-seasoned" from several areas of specialty.

Some private investor staff are recruited from the large investment banking and financial firms. Investment and commercial bankers bring a strong set of finance and financial structuring skills to these firms. These skills are important at the front-end of the life cycle of an investment where the private investor is structuring the often complex terms of their investment in the company, and in the case of an LBO/MBO the very complex debt financing and deal structuring of a go-private transaction. They are also important at the tail end of the life cycle of an investment when the private investor will be looking to either structure an acquisition or an IPO.

Private investors also hire staff with industry expertise to match their sector focus. They may hire research analysts from investment banks who have been covering the sector or "buy-side" analysts from institutional investors who have been doing the same. These people provide a deep understanding of the financials and metrics of a particular type of business, as well as generally strong financial skills. However, these people are more valuable to private equity firms working with established companies and are less likely to be found at venture capital firms dealing with early stage companies. The other type of industry specialists, which are more likely to be found at a venture capital firm, are professionals who have spent a significant time working in management of an established company in the sector. Rather than a focus on financial metrics, these people bring an expertise in the actual operation of a company in the sector. Thus, you will see that at many private investor firms, the staff has been recruited in part from major players in the relevant space. Venture capital firms focusing on technology and telecommunications may have former executes from Cisco, Microsoft or Lucent. Firms focused on entertainment businesses may pull staff from Viacom or Sony.

Somewhat related to this group are the staff that are recruited after a history in the small company end of the space. These serial entrepreneurs bring an understanding of the industry from an operational point of view but also bring an understanding of how to operate in the space as a start-up. There is a dramatic difference between developing a new product at Cisco, armed with massive resources and a pre-built customer channel, and building that same product in a "garage" while trying to knock on customer doors with a business card no one recognizes. The industry entrepreneur brings a different skill set than the big company industry executive. For obvious reasons, venture capital firms tend to focus on this kind of background for their staff. When they want to keep their staff lean and simply have a resource they can use to insert into a good company with a weak management team, they will keep a stable of "entrepreneurs in residence" that are compensated largely or wholly based on the performance of the single company in which they are inserted.

This combination of backgrounds provides the private investor with a nice mix of skills that they can deploy to make their initial investing decisions and subsequently in support of their portfolio companies. While these people come from a variety of backgrounds and bring different skills, they commonly share a set of personal characteristics.

Private investor staff will tend to be exceedingly hardworking and ambitious. They tend to have either been very successful in their prior careers and, particularly in the case of younger hires, have stellar academic credentials. Particularly in the last two decades, private investors have become incredibly popular places to work. This probably comes from a combination of the increased attention they've gotten in the wake of the technology boom and a realization of the incredibly high long-term compensation they are able to mete out to their staff. At the same time, the number of professionals employed by these firms remains incredibly low. The use of outside advisors like investment bankers, and the staff of the companies in which they invest, allow these firms to maintain incredible leverage ratios even as the dollar amounts they invest rise. All but the largest firms rarely employee more than 40 professionals. The result of this increasing demand and limited supply of jobs is that securing a position in one of these firms is incredibly hard to do. Only the best of the best need apply.

Staff of private investor firms usually share a passion for building and growing businesses, coupled with a love of the deal. In a sense they blend the personalities of investment bankers and other professionals heavily focused on doing deals with corporate managers and, more importantly, entrepreneurs, who love the challenge of growing a business. Unlike stock traders and research analysts, they don't view their portfolio companies as stock investments, but more as operating businesses. Certainly they always have the market in the back of their minds since this is one of the key ways they may see a liquidity event, but on a day-to-day basis they are much more focused on the strategies of improving the operations of the business. This is natural since unlike a stock trader whose position in a company is liquid and can be bought and sold day-to-day, private investors are likely to have a two to five year horizon on their investment.

The staff of a private investor have several key responsibilities. It's best to categorize them in terms of the life cycle of one of their investments, but, keep in mind that at any given time they may be performing any of these tasks since each of their investments may be at a different stage.

Deal Sourcing

You've set up your fund, you've gotten commitments of $100 million from investors, you've made up nice letterhead, now what? One of the most arduous efforts for any private investor, particularly the early stage venture capital, is finding deals. First, you have to get a pipeline of opportunities set up. This may involve relationships with other private investors, your staff's own network, or simply setting up a website and taking emails. It actually takes a lot of effort to find opportunities, but to quote an old cliché, be careful what you ask for because a deal pipeline is sort of like a river when the spring thaw comes. You can end up with an overwhelming flow, dragging a lot of flotsam and jetsam in its wake. Even a smaller private investor can receive dozens if not hundreds of proposals, pitches, inquiries and terms sheets a week. One of the major tasks of any private investor is to cull through all this material and try to trim it down to the limited number of deals that you want to seriously investigate. This is one of the reasons that private investors like to get opportunities through relationships with other private investors, large companies and personal contacts. There is a hope that these sources will have at least somewhat filtered the opportunity, at the very least removing the most wacky, bizarre and unreasonable of the lot.

A first filter will seek to find opportunities which on their face have reasonable business models with a good value proposition, realistic plans and a founder with some credibility. Usually, the first filter is done by relatively junior staff that take a massive stack and reduce it to a few candidates for further review. Of course, during the height and excitement of the technology boom in the late 1990s, many ideas that probably should have been caught by this first filter not only made it past, but all the way to dramatic levels of funding.

By 2001, investors in the technology space were becoming so dispirited with failed business models and products that generated tiny revenues after massively expensive build-outs, that there was a desperate attraction to any business with "real numbers." One day I got an email from an investment banker friend with an attached email he'd received. His note was fairly cryptic. "Take a look at this business proposal. Good solid numbers." The attachment was a well-written professional summary of a business that was looking for a round of venture capital funding. Though they were vague about the exact nature of the business beyond saying it was a "consumer service" they were very clear on an established financial model with good margins and a stable and growing revenue base. The numbers sounded great and the pitch was professional and reasonable. This was a dramatic contrast to the flowery and ridiculous "Microsoft in five years" technology pitches I'd been reading. Then came the punch line. The pitch ended with a link to their site for a description of the product offering......they were escort services. I had to laugh. My friend had tempted me with "old economy" numbers from the ultimate old economy business. Sadly we couldn't invest, even though the margins looked great.

Due Diligence
Due diligence is a term of art that basically means researching and investigating a company or entity. There are many forms of due diligence

and different players take the lead on each. Later in the book we'll review some of the major advisor-players like lawyers and investment bankers and each has a role in a deal's due diligence exercise. Here I will focus on the due diligence which is unique to a private investor.

Private investors in public companies – those doing LBO/MBO transactions – have the luxury of relying heavily on the public documents and audited financials of a company. By contrast, private investors working with a private company must be far more wary about both the operations and financials of the company, and develop a strong understanding of the company's business model and the industry. When evaluating a private company, particularly an early stage or start-up company, the private investor must understand a myriad of issues including the product, technology, go-to-market and pricing strategy, management and staff, partners and suppliers, competitors, barriers to entry and financial projections, but the first order of business for a private investor is to establish the very basic viability of a business. Unlike investors in large established companies, private investors in early stage and developing companies have to ask the most basic questions. Does the product or service work? Does anyone want to buy it? Does someone else already sell something like it? Can we make money selling it? Due diligence for an early stage company starts by determining whether the business exists at all before getting onto the subsequent issue of how attractive and valuable the business is. This is one of the reasons that private investors value industry operational expertise. Only people with experience running a business in the sector can ask the right questions to identify whether a business is sound.

Valuation
Once due diligence has established that the business is worthwhile and the private investor is interested, they need to establish the value of the business. It's important to note that there are two particular points in time when this measure is estimated, the point of investment and the point of a liquidity event when the investment is sold off. For some people looking at a company the second point isn't that important – a good example would be a

Strategic Investor who never plans to sell but is buying the business to integrate with their own. But for private investors, it is the difference between these two numbers that represents their gain. The value of a business to a private investor is not just how much it's worth today but also what they think it will be worth in the two to six year time horizon they have for the investment.

We'll have a more detailed discussion of valuation methods when we discuss investment bankers, but in general terms, this is the exercise of determining what a company or business is worth. For private equity firms this is a fairly quantitative exercise and as we will discuss below, there are a good set of established tools and metrics for determining value, but for angels and venture capitalists dealing with early stage companies this exercise is a lot more art than science. In a company with either no revenue or a very volatile and uncertain financial future, it is hard to choose numbers upon which everyone agrees, to drive a valuation. Inevitably, the entrepreneur will envision the classic "hockey stick" where his currently deminimus, or non-existent, revenues, grow at astronomical rates right after he gets funding. During the height of the technology boom in 2000, it was not unusual for me to get valuation proposals from small technology companies with such hockey stick projections. I was always particularly entertained by projections that, if you carried them to their mathematical conclusion, would have a company with two employees and no existing revenues, growing to the size of Microsoft in five years. While this is theoretically possible, I guess, I was fairly sure it wasn't going to happen to any, and certainly not to all, of the dozens of companies that presented me with such a scenario. By contrast to this exuberant optimism, to quote everyone's favorite central banker, the private investor will try to moderate expectations to make it as likely as possible that her investment will yield a return. The valuation exercise for an early stage company usually starts with a dramatically broad bid-ask spread between the expectations of the company and those of the investor, and then involves a delicate negotiation based on opinion, speculation and ultimately power and leverage, rather than financial calculation.

Negotiating/Structuring Investment

The negotiation and structuring of an investment is particularly complex and challenging for a private investor. Unless the business is being taken private in an LBO/MBO, there is unlikely to be a clear valuation, and in most cases the private investor has a certain amount of leverage since the company is in need of funding to grow, or even just survive. Unlike other counterparties like strategic investors, private investors make their money based on the arbitrage between the value now and later, and go through these negotiations on a regular basis. As a result, it's no surprise that private investors are notorious for being exceedingly hard negotiators. Among the variables, beyond basic price, introduced into a negotiation include warrants, options and other mechanisms for private investors to increase their stake, control through board positions and special veto rights, preferential rights on any future equity offering or IPO, and preferential rights to recoup their investment if the company's value declines. [28]

Beyond maximizing value and the natural inclination to negotiate hard, there's a good reason that private investors are so aggressive at the deal table. While we may recognize the inherent value of their expertise and network of relationships, the only thing of undeniable, absolute and definite value that they bring is money. They are in a position of dramatically greater power before making an investment.

After their money is in the hands of management, the leverage of a private investor declines precipitously. It's not surprising that they try to get as many preferential terms in the legal documents since post-closing they may have to depend on those terms for protection as their perceived power declines.

---

28 The terms of a venture capital/private equity investment are, in and of themselves, the subject of many books and the focus of an entire sub-specialty of lawyers. For a more detailed discussion of venture capital terms sheets, see Wilmerding, Alex, Term Sheets & Valuations: An Inside Look at the Intricacies of Term Sheets & Valuations, (Aspatore 2001), Wilmerding, Alex, Deal Terms: The Finer Points of Deal Structures, Valuations, Term Sheets, Stock Options and Getting Deals Done, (Aspatore 2002) and Levin, Jack, Structuring Venture Capital, Private Equity, and Entrepreneurial Transactions: 2003 (Aspen 2003).

Board Sitting and Network/Support
We've already discussed the role of post-investment support that private investors provide including a seat on the board where they can provide their expertise and experience, and help through both their portfolio company and personal network. On a day-to-day basis, this means a lot of regular and personal contact with management. A big part of what private investors do is to maintain that contact through phone calls, meeting and emails. Some management teams embrace this relationship and seek them out. Others are not so enthusiastic and the private investor has to be more assertive. Working closely with the company is not only a way to add value to the private investor's investment, but also the most effective way for them to monitor it. As we noted before, it is challenging to assess the status of a non-public company, and it is just as difficult to keep track of its progress unless you have a close personal touch with management.

Liquidity Event Management
The liquidity event is where the rubber meets the road for the private investor; this is where they get paid. It is all the more dramatic an event, since for every successful portfolio company there are many failures, and thus a liquidity event is often a dramatic turn of events financially for the private investor. I'm sure that the day a company like Yahoo went public the personal financial fortunes of many private investors were made. It's therefore no surprise that private investors are deeply and firmly involved in the decision to trigger a liquidity event and its execution. From reviewing alternatives and quantifying them, to choosing advisors and partners, to executing the transaction and determining the terms, the private investor will be a loud voice and in some cases may take the lead, depending in part on the size of their stake and level of control they wield. Private investors will often be the ones to identify a potential acquirer and even make contact and gauge interest. This serves an additional purpose since it gives the management team a certain amount of distance and "plausible deniability." Similarly, private investors will closely monitor both the financial performance of the company and the public markets, waiting for an optimal window to emerge for an IPO. If an IPO is pursued they will be heavily

involved with the process and are often instrumental in choosing the investment bankers and lawyers for the deal. Again here there is a secondary benefit since they tend to have strong relationships with these advisors and tend to be repeat players, and thus may be in a better position than management to dictate strong terms.

While there are distinct benefits to this level of involvement by the private investor, there are also significant pitfalls. While management and the board of directors must represent the interests of all shareholders, private investors focus on their own interests. Where the two diverge, management will be put in the difficult position of having to face off against their largest shareholders, and often their early benefactors, who might be credited with giving them the funding to make the company successful in the first place. In this regard there's also an interesting inherent legal conflict when it comes to board positions held by private investors. In theory, any board member owes a fiduciary duty to ALL shareholders, but if a board member is an employee of a particular private investor they will clearly tend to favor that firm's interests.

You might ask why the interests of a private investor might differ from that of other investors. There are a variety of different permutations and situations but let me give you one example. If we have a private investor who invested in an early round at a very low valuation, and who is now under great pressure from its funders to show positive results, it might be strongly inclined to drive to a liquidity event like the sale of the company to a large competitor. If management believes that the price offered by the competitor is far less than it will be able to get in another year, once (for example) its new product is launched, they would be inclined to reject the offer. These situations are actually quite common and you often see private investors at odds with management, and even with other private investors from different funding rounds (who bought in on different terms) over whether to pursue a particular liquidity event.

4.   Private Investors: Economic Model and Their Incentives/Biases

We've already covered the basics of the private investor economic model. It's a fairly simple proposition. Private investors build up a fund of capital, usually from a number of large institutional investors and massively wealthy individuals. They then put that capital to use in a portfolio of investments. In general, they expect some of the portfolio companies to falter, others to do marginally well and a few to be home runs. The ratio between these three outcomes and the breadth of extremes between them varies based on the type of private investor. At one extreme are the angels and the very early stage venture capitalists. They are investing in the financial equivalent of long shots, barely more than an idea on paper in some cases, but in the rare instance where a company takes off, the return is astronomical. A typical early stage venture capital firm might expect that for every twenty investments it makes, perhaps fourteen will entirely fail, another four might be break-even or be modest gainers, but the remaining two will be huge wins. For an early stage venture capital firm, a return of 1,000 percent or even 10,000 percent is not unrealistic for these rare winners. As you travel up the maturity scale from early stage venture capital to late stage venture capital and toward mezzanine financing, the risk of a total loss goes down but the upside reduces as well. For example, we might imagine a hypothetical technology company that does three rounds of financing prior to going public. In the first round they sell 25 percent of the company at a $1 million pre-money valuation. In the second round they sell another 25 percent at a $10 million valuation. In the third round they sell a final 25 percent at a $50 million valuation. Finally, they have a liquidity event with an IPO that values the company at $100 million. Here's how the returns would break out:

Round	Valuation	Amount Invested	Stake	Final Value of Stake	Return on Investment
Angel	$ 1,000,000	$ 250,000	25%	$ 25,000,000	9900%
Venture Capital - A Round	$ 10,000,000	$ 2,500,000	25%	$ 25,000,000	900%
Venture Capital - B Round	$ 50,000,000	$ 12,500,000	25%	$ 25,000,000	100%

Keep in mind that while the angel in this example makes a dramatically higher return, for every company that goes from angel round to A round, or from A round to B round or from B round to IPO, there are many that falter along the way. As the valuation rises so, theoretically, does the chance that the company will succeed.

Private equity firms invest in companies that are either very well established private companies, or public companies they are taking private. As a result, the risk of a total loss of investment is much smaller but on the flip side, the chance of a dramatic increase in value is also small. In a sense you can think of private investing as running along a continuum of volatility (in both the upside and downside), from very high-risk start-ups to large established public or barely pre-public companies.

Regardless of the level of risk or the stage of the investment, all private investors follow the same fundamental model. They take a large equity stake in a business, they help make changes or improvements as well as adding capital, and then they sell their stake to recognize a return. The two primary liquidity events that allow them to recognize that return are Strategic Transactions and IPOs. While there are some cases where they may be able to sell their stake to another private investor, or even to the founders or management, this is relatively rare. The result is that private investors are very focused on driving toward one of these two liquidity events.

Management's compensation comes through a combination of the eventual upside of a liquidity event and regular compensation, but private investors are only paid at the endgame. While it varies from firm to firm, most private investors have a time horizon of no longer than five or six years for making their exit. They are driven not only by the incentive to recognize personal gains, but also by the need to show returns to their funding sources. To a certain extent, a private investor's business model is a spiral of success or failure. Showing good returns leads to more funding which in turn drives up the size of the investments they can make. While private investors often also receive management fees which allow them to cover costs and pay their staff base salaries, the real money is made through their personal equity interests in the deals and more importantly, failure to show performance will cause funds to dry up which in turn would dry up their management fees (which are usually a small percentage of the total funds under management).

How hard a private investor will push to trigger a liquidity event is also affected by the state of its total portfolio. In a market where the private investor has been showing good returns and is under little pressure from funding sources, it may be willing to delay a liquidity event in hopes of getting a greater return, but in a market where the private investor's other portfolio companies are falling by the wayside, it will be under significant pressure to cash out of a successful one quickly and show a tangible return.

5. Management of, or Interaction with, Private Investors

Private investors are amongst the more rational players in a Strategic Transaction. They are sophisticated deal makers, and investments and Strategic Transactions are their bread and butter. Since they are private entities they tend to be less concerned about press and public perceptions. There are tightly focused on their portfolio and its performance.

Having said that, there are some opportunities to manage a relationship with private investors. First, it is important to understand their current appetite for risk. This will depend not only on their original charter (the sector and risk level that they proposed to their funding sources) but also on the effect of the current environment. If a private investor is pressed to show financial performance it may be willing to offer more attractive terms to get a deal done quickly. Under any circumstances, a private investor is likely to be a strong ally in trying to convince management to do a deal at all. While they may push for a high price, private investors will be eager to get a deal done, and since they are regular dealmakers they are generally very adept at the logistics of the process.

Finally, private investors are often good intermediaries when trying to initiate conversations with a company. Working through them allows you to make discrete inquiries and since they have the ear of management, you may get a more serious and quick response than through a direct inquiry. Since private investors are deeply familiar with the company and its operations, they are often a good source of initial information on the company.

However, it's important to remember that at the end of the day, a private investor only has as much formal authority as they have voting power as shareholders. While they may be more active in trying to broker a Strategic Transaction, if another party like management or founders has a majority of the shares, they still have the power.

8

The Lawyers

A. Summary

We've all told our share of lawyer jokes, and the analogies to sharks and rats are plentiful, but when you are doing a Strategic Transaction, your lawyer is your friend, your counsel, your representative and perhaps most importantly, your protector. In theory, the fundamental role of lawyers is to take a business understanding reached between two parties, and turn it into a set of legally binding documents. They are scriveners, the historians of a deal, and in a business environment usually filled with "glass is half full" optimists, salesmen, entrepreneurs and dealmakers, they are the naysayers that look for the downside in every term. The devil is always in the details and lawyers are the devil's advocate.

Lawyers come in two general flavors, in-house and outside counsel. Like any other employee/consultant alternative this is like the difference between buying a car and renting one. A car you own is a big upfront cost but you get unlimited use. A rental car only costs you when you use it, but then it costs a lot more. There are other differences between in-house and outside lawyers. Typically, in-house lawyers are generalists. Unless a company is massive enough to justify a full team of specialists, it will likely have a small team of lawyers who cover the full range of legal issues. Some companies have the need for specialists based on their business model. Biotech companies will likely need an intellectual property specialist while a manufacturing company with lots of blue collar employees might need a labor and employment specialist, but few companies have enough deal flow to justify a mergers & acquisitions or investments specialist. However, in-house lawyers have another area of expertise that is crucial to any deal. They understand the company, the business and the market space. In-house lawyers will inevitably have a far better grasp of the details of a company's business than almost any outside counsel. They will understand the technology, the products, the operations and the competitive landscape. They will also have an extensive network of personal relationships with employees particularly outside the management team and in line management that is crucial to a deal.

☙ ﷽ ❧

By contrast, outside counsel may not have a deep grasp of the company's business or relationship with employees, but they bring deep specialty expertise and massive firepower in the form of manpower and resources. Most law firms employ a full range of legal specialists covering areas as diverse as tax, antitrust, contracts, securities, product liability, intellectual property and of course, mergers & acquisitions. Outside counsel brings the expertise that comes from doing one type of transaction or case over and over again. While an in-house lawyer might expect to encounter an occasional Strategic Transaction, an outside counsel specializing in mergers and acquisitions will have a track record doing dozens or even hundreds of deals. This wealth of experience can provide crucial guidance in the more complex or unusual areas of these transactions. Similarly, from a documentation point of view, an outside counsel will have standard forms of almost an infinite number of variations on deal structures, eliminating the need to "reinvent the wheel" when it comes to the arduous task of drafting hundreds of pages of deal documents. Just as important, an outside counsel firm brings the flexibility of a large legal and non-legal staff which, like an investment bank, can be pulled into a deal for peak periods. In one particular deal, early in my career, we were pushing to close the sale of a large chunk of a multi-billion dollar company. Since word had leaked to the Wall Street Journal, it became critical that the deal be closed by morning to ensure that management could tell employees personally. The idea of a unionized labor force hearing about a huge sale of a division from the newspapers was a CEO nightmare. The basic terms of the deal had been agreed to, but now we had to turn those basic terms into nearly 1000 pages of detailed legal agreements. As we sat in a conference room negotiating page by page, I had drafted a team of two junior associates, four paralegals and five word processors who sat in various empty offices and secretary's desks outside the conference room. As each page of the agreement was marked with changes and corrections by the negotiating team, it was ferried out to the waiting army who made corrections, added language, edited changes and made copies of the revised pages which were funneled back into the room and distributed to the negotiators. Literally, page-by-page, the document was changed on the fly to reflect the new terms. On another occasion, a client announced that it wanted to make a bid on a competitor and had been given only four days to review all the due diligence documents before making a bid. Within three hours, our firm had assembled a team of junior lawyers from a variety of specialties including tax, real estate, litigation and mergers and acquisitions that were on a flight that afternoon to Florida. By later that week, the team had produced a 150 page report summarizing the key points of nearly 50 boxes of documents, and the client was comfortable submitting the bid on time. Marshalling these kinds of resources to deal with the peaks in a deal is what makes outside counsel essential in many Strategic Transactions.

In this section I will make broad statements about lawyers without distinguishing between in-house and outside counsel. In reality, where the role is split between the two varies. Different companies put different levels of trust and responsibility in the hands of outside and in-house counsel. At the end of the day, together they need to produce the net results discussed below.[29]

---

[29] But it is important to note that while the inside lawyer also thinks of management as a client, she has some greater independent fiduciary duty than an outside lawyer. The general counsel of a company theoretically owes a duty to the board of directors and shareholders while outside counsel are much more pure service providers. But this issue only arises in very rare cases where the general counsel feels that management's actions are actually a violation of their fiduciary duty.

If you are doing international deals it is particularly important to note the difference between the role of lawyers in the U.S., Asia and Europe. It has become a cliché that the U.S. is a land of lawyers, but it is also very true. Lawyers and legal documents play a much greater role in American business than in European or Asian business. There is a large literature discussing the role of lawyers in various societies and countries and I won't try to recreate it here. While lawyers are highly respected and central players in American business, they are more tangential in European business, and almost sidelined in Asian business. Part of the explanation for this is the nature of trust in each society. American business is built by newcomers, entrepreneurs and garage-investors. American companies are run by a quickly cycling and changing pool of managers and executives whose tenures in their positions are getting shorter and shorter each decade. These unknowns haven't, and don't tend to, develop deep relationships and reputations in their industries as is true of the family-owned businesses, and career management, of some European and Asian companies. Therefore, the need for more formal mechanisms to enforce agreements and resolve miscommunications is greater in the United States. These differences extend more broadly to societal structures and may explain the broader differences in the role of lawyers in these societies. For our purposes it is just important to note that while American business generally involves lawyers early and deeply in a deal process, and depends on very detailed written contracts, European and Asian business tends to put less emphasis on lawyers and written documentation. However, in principal, lawyers in all countries can perform some or all of the following roles in a Strategic Transaction.

B. Lawyers: What's Their Role?

Lawyers are more versatile in Strategic Transactions than perhaps any other advisor. They have a range of roles from the most specific legal documentation to the most general advice and counsel, but throughout this exercise the hallmark of their role is that they serve as perhaps the company's only unbiased advisor.

1. Counselor and Strategic Advisor

Lawyers are called "counsel" for good reason. Of all the professions, lawyers tend to have the strongest and longest term relationship with the senior management of a company. There are few areas of business that don't require the input of a lawyer.[30] From potential litigation and deals, to everyday contracts, employment agreements and protection of intellectual property, lawyers are an essential part of turning a business goal into an actionable event. Relationships between lawyers and clients tend to have a lot of continuity. While some other advisors may only be brought in for a particular type of deal or event, lawyers tend to have long-term continuous relationships with their clients. The result is that their clients often look to them for more than purely legal advice but for general wisdom. This is particularly true for more senior lawyers who, from their peculiar vantage point, will have seen hundreds of deals and negotiations over the course of their careers. As an executive's relationship with a lawyer stretches over years, she may look to that lawyer not just for legal advice, but also as an unbiased and wise counselor on a broad range of issues. The key is lack of bias, and as we will discuss below, it is the economic model, as well as the very nature of the profession, that provides lawyers with this status.

2. Regulatory Guidance and Representation

Any company is subject to some sort of regulation, and most are subject to a variety of different sets of regulations from a variety of different sources. Again, this is an area where the U.S. may take the lead, although with the emergence of a set of European Union regulation, one might argue that the Europeans are gaining on us.

---

[30] This is truer in the United States than in some other regions of the world, particularly in Asia where lawyers are seen as much lower level functionaries and less likely to be used as representatives in negotiations.

Regulations can be driven by the location of the company and its operations, the identity of its shareholders, the nature of those operations or even the nature of its customers. This will be discussed in further detail when we talk about the regulators that enforce all those regulations, but whatever the source of regulations, companies need help both complying with the regulations and dealing with the regulators.

Regulations are complex, vague and often hard to apply to a particular fact pattern. For example, a regulation might say that you must inform customers of the contents of a product. But how do you have to inform them? In writing? On the label? Before they buy? And what level of detail do you have to use? Do you have to tell them the amount of each ingredient or just that it's in there? Lawyers help guide a company through the process of understanding regulations and figuring out how to comply with them, at the lowest cost and effort.

Then there are situations where you need to interact with regulators. You may need to communicate with them as part of a regulatory requirement; a report to the regulator. You might have questions about a vague regulation and whether it applies. Or you might want to negotiate with them. Lawyers are a company's representatives in all these discussions. One great example is the approval of an offering document by which a company registers securities it intends to sell to the public – an IPO for instance. Usually, a company makes an initial filing of a draft of the registration statement and the SEC makes comments. The comments could include a request for more information or even request changes to the language. In many cases, these changes make the document less attractive as a selling document and a negotiation ensues with the company's lawyers arguing with the SEC for a more moderate position. For instance, there is a section in each registration statement called the *Risk Factors* which is supposed to identify to potential investors the major risks of an investment in the company. If a hamburger chain (the next McDonalds, let's call them Big Burger Buddy) were trying to go public, the SEC might ask for a risk factor stating that in the event of an outbreak of mad cow disease in the U.S., revenues could decline dramatically. Lawyers for Big Burger Buddy would argue to the SEC that since there hasn't been a documented outbreak of mad cow disease in the U.S., this is too remote and unlikely to be a reasonable risk factor and shouldn't be required in the document. For every registration statement there may be literally dozens of such points discussed between lawyers and the SEC.

Lawyers thus help companies not only understand and comply with regulations but try to ease the pain of doing so by helping them plan for compliance, figure out how to do it, and in some cases negotiate with regulators to lessen the burden. In a Strategic Transaction, this exercise becomes particularly crucial since in many cases such regulations are not merely "check the box" exercises but may actually determine whether a deal is blocked or allowed to be completed.

3. Due Diligence

We've talked about due diligence in several contexts, and clearly lawyers don't take the lead in figuring out what a business does or how much it is worth, but indirectly they are the foundation of any due diligence exercise. Remember that a company is simply a legal entity, and the things it owns and operates are also based on legal rights and obligations. So any assessment of a company makes assumptions about its legal status, legal rights and legal obligations. This is where the lawyers come in. Legal due diligence is a huge subject and I won't attempt to do it justice in this small section. I'll simply provide a basic idea of how it is important to a deal.[31]

When doing a Strategic Transaction you must first establish that you want to do the deal, but then, it is equally crucial to establish that what you are going to get after the dust settles is what you think you're going to get. Legal

---

[31] There are many books that discuss legal due diligence. What follows is a small selection that I believe are particularly accessible to the non-lawyer. Lajoux, Alexandra and Elson, Charles, The Art of M&A Due Diligence (McGraw-Hill Trade 2000); Camp, Justin, Venture Capital Due Diligence: A Guide to Making Smart Investment Choices and

due diligence is the – often extensive – process of reviewing the legal documentation of a company to ensure that there is no difference between those two. Lawyers will look at the ownership documents to make sure the people selling you the company actually own it (not as certain as you might think). Lawyers will look at the agreements and contracts the company has since if you buy it you may be stepping into these legal obligations.[32] This is true of both assets (customer contracts, monies owed) and liabilities (debts, obligations to suppliers and customers). Similarly the lawyers will ensure that nothing the company has signed interferes with its ability to do the deal with you.

The legal due diligence exercise is a lengthy and arduous one. It generally involves looking through dozens or even hundreds of boxes of documents. In the case of a partnership or joint venture, rather than a full acquisition, the exercise is much lighter but you still need to review documents that might affect the ability of the partner to execute their obligations and to ensure they have the rights and assets necessary to do so.

Legal due diligence usually involves a number of junior lawyers sitting for hours or days on end, often in a conference room at the counterparty's offices, reviewing documents and taking notes. Since the documents are usually highly confidential, it is relatively rare for a company to be willing to send copies. Perhaps more importantly they are usually too voluminous for this to be practical. It is cheaper to fly three people to Houston for a week than to copy (under controlled conditions to ensure confidentiality) forty boxes of documents.

Increasing Your Portfolio Returns (John Wiley & Sons 2002); and Due Diligence for Corporate Acquisitions (Aspen).

[32] Strategic Transactions can be structured so that such legal obligations are included or excluded. However, even when they're excluded, as in an asset purchase, there is still the potential for them to affect the buyer in a variety of ways including subsequent litigation, and security interests granted in the assets being purchased. More importantly, the buyer will often want to step into these obligations since they may be highly valuable, as in the case of customer contracts or well negotiated supply contracts with good terms. In any case, a thorough review of legal obligations, contracts and rights will be essential.

The key to effective legal due diligence is to ensure that the lawyers understand the business priorities underlying the deal. This ensures that they focus their efforts appropriately. For example, if a company is being acquired largely for its customer relationships, with the plan of abandoning its current product line and transitioning the customers to a different product, the lawyers shouldn't spend too much time on the intellectual property rights to the technology, which is likely to end up on the trash heap. Instead they should be scouring the customer contracts for such things as the right to terminate upon a change in control, or triggers to a change in pricing. Lawyers who understand the business drivers of a deal will be more efficient and produce due diligence that better protects their clients. As we can see, this will be a common theme of lawyer management in other areas as well.

Negotiations

The preparation, the calculations and the machinations all lead up to this moment. When people think of deals and Strategic Transactions they think of this, the deal table. To be clear, all negotiations don't take place around a big mahogany table. They take place over dinner, in small conference rooms, and primarily over email and over the phone. A negotiation usually happens in fits and starts over a period of time. Nonetheless, it is the heart of a deal and the relatively short period of time during which an agreement is either reached, or fails. Even in industries and situations where valuation and pricing is highly mathematical and there is lots of data, massive amounts of money can shift from one party to the other in the course of a negotiation. The myriad of other smaller items that are part of a negotiation are often as important as the purchase price itself. The devil is in the details, and from legal representations and warranties, to the currency used for the purchase price, to collars, earn-outs and other price protections, there are a variety of terms in any deal that can have a material impact on the effective value paid and received.

The real challenge of any negotiation is not only that there are numerous individual issues, but that they all interact and intersect with each other. The strategy of negotiation must involve balancing different issues against each other and trying to get the best overall package of terms. This is one of the areas where lawyers have a chance to shine. Corporate lawyers are natural negotiators since even the simplest agreement or contract has multiple points of potential disagreement, so in any deal, no matter how simple, behind the scenes lawyers are negotiating with each other dozens of times. When they come to a really big deal, with very important terms, the process of negotiation comes naturally to lawyers. As you might expect, this is where the most senior lawyers get actively involved. Not only is this perhaps the most challenging part of a lawyer's role, and one where experience is invaluable, but it also has the highest visibility in front of the client, and the greatest opportunity for both glory and major mistakes.

Lawyers are also usually able to approach the negotiation in a uniquely rational and unemotional state. This is particularly important since often parties to a deal can get stuck on issues for personal reasons, and end up not maximizing the real value of the deal. For example, if I'm buying a company and the seller/founder refuses to sign a representation or warranty saying that he actually has contracts with his customers, I could get mad. I'd think this was unreasonable and either suggest he was being difficult for no reason or that he was an idiot to have that little a grip over his business. However, my lawyer might point out that since his standard contract is terminable at will by the customer, it really isn't that important. When I call each customer after the deal, I could just have them sign a new contract and I wouldn't be much worse off since even if there was a signed contract in place, they could have walked away from it anyway. One important role of lawyers in a negotiation is to remind their client of what really matters.

Lawyers are also very good at managing the process of a negotiation. Negotiations can take place over a period of time in the form of dozens of emails and calls and several in-person meetings. Just keeping track of what's been agreed to, what's still open to discussion, what we care about, and what we are saving as a "give-away," is a complex task. In a standard acquisition agreement, the two parties might initially find 100 or 200 different points on which to disagree and each one needs to be negotiated and concluded.

Finally, lawyers play an important buffer role by taking the lead in negotiations. These processes tend to get fairly hostile at times, even during the friendliest deal. Each side may make threats to walk away from the table and try to play hardball, but in many cases it's important for the two counterparties to maintain a good relationship. Whether it's because this is a business deal after which they will have to work together or because they are likely to encounter each other in the market again, they may want to distance themselves from the conflict. Lawyers take that front role and take the brunt of each side's anger, simultaneously trying to get the best deal for their client while allowing their client to remain above the fray. Here's a good illustration. During my time as an attorney I represented an investment bank that was serving as the underwriter for a Fortune 500 company's equity offering. We had asked the company's lawyers if they would make a certain representation in the document and they had said no. Further they had said this was a company policy and not open to negotiation. When I told my client, he insisted that I bring it up again, and the agitated company counsel repeated that it was not on the table for discussion. That afternoon we had a conference call with the company, investment bank and both law firms. My client decided he wanted to send a subtle message to the company that he and his firm had been very flexible on terms of the deal and it had been hard to deal with their lawyers – to get some brownie points and credit with the company, and here's how he did it. On this big conference call he raised the issue of the representation again. The company counsel went absolutely ballistic. He began screaming at the top of his lungs that he had already told "[expletive] Frankel" that this was not on the table and that if "[expletive] Frankel" hadn't told the bank, that was his fault. At the end of the tirade my client apologized and said he hadn't known about this, but that he understood their point, though on another point (which he thought he had a chance of getting) he was hoping they could show some flexibility. He won this other point. Note how each party avoided direct conflict. My client used me to agitate the other side without doing it himself. The company counsel directed his bile at me to avoid having a bad relationship with my client.

4. Documentation

If the devil is in the details, the legal documentation of a deal is chock full of Satan. This is something that even some sophisticated executives don't fully appreciate. Particularly in a litigious country like the United States, a deal is limited to what you write down on paper. The result is that you only bought, sold, promised or were promised what is actually written in the deal documents. Clumsy or weak drafting of those documents creates the potential that you won't get what you think you got. As a deal is being negotiated, it is simultaneously being documented. At the initial stages of a deal you may draft a term sheet. This is supposed to represent the basic outline of an agreement, but until you have a full and complete deal document you don't actually have a final deal to execute. "Full and complete" is not an understatement. These documents are massive and complex. It is not unusual for a merger or acquisition agreement to top 100 pages, along with literally hundreds of additional pages in schedules and exhibits. This is generally the work of mid-level lawyers, senior enough to understand and be trusted with the work, but not senior enough to pawn it off on their staff.

These lawyers are the silent overseers of a deal. They work with their clients, they do due diligence and at the end of the day they are tasked with producing a document that embodies the intentions of the parties. In this age of litigation, the lawyer drafting the agreement needs to not only document the deal that has been reached but also plan for a broad range of contingencies and address them in the document. For example, if I'm buying a tire manufacturing plant from another company, what if, prior to closing, the plant catches fire? What if spilled chemicals are discovered under the plant after the deal is closed? Or even worse, what if a chemical leakage that the seller allowed but wasn't at that time illegal, is made illegal after I buy the plant? The lawyer not only has to document what is, but what might be.

The need to specifically document a deal is what requires lawyers to have a full and detailed understanding of not only the intended deal, but of the companies and/or assets that are subject to the deal. Just as with due diligence, a lawyer can only draft a deal document effectively if they understand the facts, as well as their client's goals and "hot buttons." At the end of the day, documenting a deal can be an arduous and unglamorous task but it is the essential step in turning a gentleman's agreement into a legally binding transaction.

5. *Technicalities of Closing*

If drafting the documents for a deal is unglamorous, the technicalities of closing are downright pedestrian. When most businesspeople think of a closing, they think of that one hour they spend in a crowded law firm conference room, signing what seem to be a ridiculous number of signature pages. This is quickly followed by a departure to a restaurant for dinner, drinks and celebratory pats on the back, but like the pictures of a small hump rising from Loch Ness, this is just the tip of the iceberg. Along with the main deal document, most deals require many additional supporting legal documents and exhibits to be prepared in advance of the closing. In the same fashion as it has been done for decades, multiple copies of each document are assembled in a room and carefully examined to make sure they're complete and ready for signing. Often, the signing has to be timed to coincide with the transfer of money or securities. All of these details are the work of junior lawyers that generally are toiling long hours, days in advance, and then gathering up the material and "picking up the pieces" for hours afterwards. It is amazing to think that even in this age of technology, massive deals are still consummated with piles of photocopied pages signed in ink.

C. Lawyers: The People and What They Do

I'll be brief in this section since much of this has been covered above. Let's begin with where lawyers come from. Unlike most other players at the deal table, there is a single font from which lawyers flow, and they follow a fairly predictable career path. Most lawyers attend law school either right after college or fairly soon thereafter, graduating in their mid or late twenties. While a few may have short clerkships with judges, most corporate lawyers go directly from law school to a law firm. Law firms are generally operated as private partnerships which means that there are two distinct classes, partners (who have an equity interest) and all other employees.

Since the law is fairly focused on credentials, where you go to law school has a lot to do with where you start work. Lawyers at the large corporate firms are most likely from the top schools, or are the absolute top students at strong second tier schools. They have worked hard through school and usually even harder at law school. They tend to be "nose to the grindstone" people with strong self-discipline and ambition, but unlike some of their MBA compatriots, their strengths tend, though there are notable exceptions, to come not from their social or sales skills but from their ability to think, write and argue. Once at a law firm, there is a fairly strict hierarchy with lawyers rising in the associate ranks explicitly based on years of service (a "first year associate" or a "fifth year associate") until they are either made, or passed over, for partnership. While young lawyers are compensated well, the compensation curve is somewhat odd. They begin with a very high salary which then increases fairly slowly year to year, but if they make partner it leaps up again.

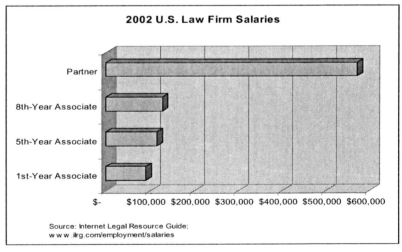

Associates who are gunning for partnership, face a nearly decade-long trudge up the hill toward the go-no-go decision of partnership, and a long and steep hill it is. Associates at the large New York law firms generally work 60-90 hours per week and the pace does not slacken much as they get more senior.

The work of a corporate lawyer varies substantially with their level of seniority.[33] Junior associates spend most of their time on the more basic tasks of due diligence, review of documents, drafting very basic documents and schedules, and a lot of process management. Senior associates are more focused on drafting primary deal documents and managing junior associates. They also take a lead role in the lower profile negotiations. On occasion, the obligations of substantive negotiation and process management can come into conflict. I once found myself working with a partner on a very large Strategic Transaction, representing the seller in an auction. We were in final negotiations and the pressure was on to close the deal. I found myself sitting in a conference room filled with senior executives and lawyers from both sides. I was the senior associate on the selling side and so I "owned" the document. As we negotiated each term, I frantically marked up the document and sent it out to be retyped. During one lull, as the clock passed from PM to AM hours, I was deeply focused on turning my notes into legal language. Everyone else in the room was chatting quietly and basically waiting for me to turn the document. The senior associate on the other side must have been feeling a bit insecure since his team was far more "top heavy" and he had been reduced to basically watching in silence. As I raced to get the document done, he spoke up. "Hey Mike, can we get some more diet cokes in here?" As the only associate from the "host firm," it was technically my job as was all other parts of process management. However, this lawyer's client, a mid-50s general counsel who was unaccustomed to being up this late and starting to show it, had come to a realization. The only thing standing between him and putting this deal, and as a result himself, to bed, was my drafting. He turned to the associate from his outside law firm and growled, "will you shut the [expletive] up." This was a situation

---

[33] I'm focusing here on corporate lawyers since they are primarily responsible for Strategic Transactions. But other specialists will be discussed below and the nature of their role and work is obviously somewhat different.

where substantive work could take precedence over process management, but in most cases a young associate will have to get both done.

Partners spend a large amount of their time doing business development and serving as senior advisors to their clients, as well as leading high profile negotiations. Whether it's on the golf course or over the phone, law firm partners spend a lot of time having general conversations and giving broad advice to clients. In many cases this may not even be legal advice, but is the general exercise of becoming a trusted advisor so the client will treat the partner, and her firm, as the default source of legal services. I've found that most partners still cherish the moments when they're called in for some particularly complex legal issue or asked to review a particularly difficult piece of drafting done by one of their associates.

D. Lawyers: Economic Model and Their Incentives/Biases

Law firms generally charge on a pure hourly rate.[34] While these hourly rates certainly are high, they fundamentally limit how much a law firm can make on a deal. Unlike the investment bankers, the revenue of the lawyers isn't tied to a particular outcome of the deal. They get paid whether or not the deal is done. This structure is supposed to create an incentive for the lawyers to be totally unbiased in advising their clients since they have no financial stake in the outcome of the deal.

That is not to say that the lawyers aren't well paid. A top New York law firm will charge rich rates for their attorney's time. Major New York law firms can charge $200-$350/hour for junior associates, $350-$500/hour for senior associates, and $500-$800/hour (or more) for partners. Of course the law firm also passes on a variety of related costs including meals, travel,

---

[34] There are some notable exceptions to this. First, I am not including in this group litigators who take on law suits on a contingency basis. I'm also not including a small and rare group of corporate firms who have been able to negotiate large deal success fees. Wachtell, Lipton was known to do this on occasion, but it remains extremely rare.

document production and support staff time, all at a rich mark-up.[35] So while law firms are charging in small incremental chunks compared to investment banks, those chunks add up. Part of the reason for this is that the hourly billing rate naturally drives an hourly billing culture at these firms. The business model of a law firm is fairly simple. By far the greatest cost is labor, primarily the lawyers. This is a fixed cost with some variability for modest year-end bonuses (in law firms bonuses are generally no more than 10%-30% of annual compensation), while revenue is variable based on hours billed. It's no surprise then that there is tremendous pressure on lawyers, particularly non-partners, to bill a huge number of hours. In the top New York law firms, during a boom market when work is readily available, it is not unusual to find young associates billing well over 3000 hours a year. Even if you assume that these associates are working so hard that they bill almost every hour they're in the office, this still equates to an average of well over sixty hours per week – more if you assume any vacation at all. In practice, in order to bill 3000 hours in a year an associate will probably average more like seventy-five hours per week.

There are some minor variations on this theme. On occasion, a firm will write down or discount a bill, in negotiation with a client, particularly if it is a strong client relationship or if the market is weak. Similarly the law firm often gets additional revenue from a client in the form of retainer fees or a success bonus. However, for the most part, the law firm business model is one of hourly incremental billing.

The economic model for the individual lawyers is also fairly simple. They make a fairly clear "deal with the devil." In exchange for very high compensation (though there are a few other professions like investment

<hr>

[35] . These mark-ups were actually the subject of a notorious article in 1991 entitled "Skaddenomics" referring to one of the biggest New York corporate firms, Skadden, Arps. In the article, the author pointed to examples of extreme mark-ups, particularly of incidentals, by a number of big law firms. The $7 bagel became famous as an example of billing excesses. Since then, firms have become more cautious about such mark ups, fearing that the wrath of their clients will well exceed the incremental revenue. Beck,

banking that are materially higher), extremely good training (although arguably some of it is just through massive volume of work) and a chance to make partner, these lawyers work extremely long and stressful hours. Those that stay and make partner are given an annuity of sorts since, once made partners, their jobs are fairly secure and compensation becomes very rich, and those that leave before coming up for partner or after failing to make it, leave with a pedigree that often allows them to move to well paying jobs as in-house lawyers, or with other law firms.

E. Management of, or Interaction with, Lawyers

The good news is that lawyers are fairly unbiased and usually only have a single ulterior motive – to bill more hours. The challenge is to manage that bias and, more importantly, the other negative effects it may have. Lawyers' tendency to consider worst case scenarios and every detail, coupled with an hourly billing rate, can lead lawyers to either over-engineer a transaction and make things overly complex, or to overwork a problem or issue. It is important to manage lawyers by establishing clear goals and expectations about the level of effort required. One example is due diligence. Without guidance a lawyer will apply an equal and extreme level of rigor to all topics of due diligence, but in some cases, some items may be relatively unimportant and making that clear to the lawyers may not only save you money in legal fees but also speed a process forward.

Similarly, it's important to keep in mind that lawyers are by their nature focused on issues like the potential for litigation, extreme clarity in terms, detailed documentation, and removing risk. They are not focused on upside issues – that's the job of their clients. As a result they will tend to focus on risks and may not be particularly good at quantifying or even identifying the offsetting benefits, or the limits of actual damage from the risk. For example, I have seen a lawyer become greatly concerned in due diligence because he could not locate an executed copy of a purported license for an Oracle database. He wanted to have the seller put extensive representations in the agreement concerning the validity of the license, but from a business point of view, I realized that (a) the cost of a new Oracle license would be small, (b) we could probably negotiate with Oracle to add the newly acquired company onto our existing license at little cost and (c) the chance that they would bother faking an Oracle license was fairly small. The lawyer saw a missing contract and a potential liability, while I saw a problem that was less than 0.01 percent of the deal size and easily fixable even if the contract never materialized. It's important to help lawyers understand the business context so that they can properly weight the real world financial impact of the legal issues they identify.

F. Variations

So far we've talked about the general corporate lawyer, but there are of course a number of variations or spins on this role as well as specialists. I'll take a moment to discuss some of the peculiarities of these different variants.

1. Seller's Counsel

Seller's counsel usually has the heaviest and most difficult job in a Strategic Transaction. Though the seller may do some basic due diligence on the buyer, particularly if they're being paid in stock, usually the buyer does a far more exhaustive review of the seller's business and documentation. Thus, seller's counsel usually has a lot more work to prepare material and documentation for review by the buyer's lawyers.

Similarly, unless this is a pure one-on-one negotiation, seller's counsel is likely to be dealing with multiple buyers at the same time, effectively multiplying the work in many areas like negotiation. In the most extreme example, the seller may be conducting a formal auction and the seller's counsel could find themselves having to simultaneously provide due diligence and then negotiate definitive documents with multiple parties.

Seller's counsel is also more likely to encounter conflicts of interest that they need to manage. Since the sale of a company is a final and decisive event, you are more likely to see management, the board and shareholders at odds. Seller's counsel is often the referee in these matters. Similarly, the seller in a transaction is more likely to need to seek shareholder approval, a very lawyer, and document, intensive activity.

The lawyers representing the seller are also in an interesting economic position. They are working on a deal that by definition will deprive them of a client and thus, helping to bring about the demise of a valuable relationship. While a seller's counsel might hope to impress the buyer with her skill, it remains unlikely that after selling the company she will be retained by the buyer, who already has its own legal counsel. Nonetheless there is a potential conflict of interest, though mild, to the extent that the seller's counsel tries to "go easy" on the buyer to curry its favor.

2. Buyer's Counsel

Buyer's counsel gets the opposite end of the economic outcome since her client will be the surviving entity, and will have grown larger, presumably meaning the potential for more legal work. This also means that there is an issue of survival that doesn't haunt seller's counsel as much. In the wake of a Strategic Transaction, particularly if paid in cash, the seller disappears and seller's counsel is unlikely to have to revisit the deal, but if anything goes wrong, any mistakes are found, any miscalculations made, they will come back to haunt the buyer and their lawyer. For example, if buyer's counsel fails to review a customer agreement and after closing the customer exercises a heretofore unknown termination clause, the value of what the buyer just purchased goes down, and buyer's counsel could be blamed. Failure to discover something in due diligence is just one example. As I've discussed, part of a lawyer's job is to try to predict every possible event, but that effort is never perfect. If the legal documents drafted don't protect against a negative outcome, no matter how unlikely, that actually comes to pass, buyer's counsel will likely be blamed.

Even if buyer's counsel doesn't have to prepare much due diligence material or deal with multiple counterparties, in many cases buyer's counsel (who may be a larger and more sophisticated firm) may sometimes take the lead in drafting the key deal documents. This makes sense since most of the terms in a purchase agreement are there to protect the buyer rather than the seller. Particularly if the deal is done in cash, most sellers are almost entirely concerned with just getting paid.

3. Advisor/Underwriter Counsel

In many deals, there is a third material player: the advisor/underwriter. I will discuss investment bankers in the next section, but in basic terms, investment bankers advise companies on Strategic Transactions and may also underwrite the issuance of securities used to fund the deal. In both these roles, investment banks take on legal obligations and risks and thus need legal advice. When a bank is simply advising a client, the role of their lawyers is fairly limited. They will review the fee agreements and the fairness opinion, but beyond that will have a limited role. This is really the extent of the risk that the bankers are incurring, and since in most cases both those documents are fairly standardized and in the case of fairness opinions the standard is adhered to religiously, there is little for them to do.

However, when a bank becomes an underwriter the picture changes dramatically. As an underwriter, the investment bank stands between the company issuing securities and the institutional and individual investors buying the securities. While they may effectively pre-sell the securities avoiding any transactional risk, technically they are buying securities and then reselling them. The result is that they need to do the same level of due diligence (if not more) that they would if they were the end-purchaser. This is since (a) there is the theoretical risk that they could end up holding the securities, but also, and more importantly (b) that since they are selling to the end-investors, they can be held liable for inaccuracies in the selling documents (the prospectus). In an underwritten deal, underwriter's counsel takes a fairly heavy role in reviewing the offering documents for the securities and ensuring that proper due diligence is done on the company.

One saving grace for underwriter's counsel is that in most cases (notably not an IPO), the issuing company is already public and so there is a lot of information already disclosed in public filings as well as auditors' opinions which can be relied upon. Nonetheless, an underwriter's counsel has a fair amount of work to do.

In both cases, but particularly in the case of underwriter's counsel, the lawyers must manage a fundamental conflict. On the one hand, they need to be rigorous in their due diligence and their negotiation since they are representing the investment bank as a counterparty to the company, buying their securities. At the same time, since the company chose the bank and has the flexibility to change that choice, they must treat the company as a client. These two goals will often come into conflict as the lawyers push for greater legal protections and more due diligence disclosure, and often the company will put pressure on the investment bankers to reign in their lawyers. This is why in-house investment bank lawyers sometimes need to take a more active role to protect the interests of the bank as a whole, versus the sales goals of a particular banker excited about a particular deal.

One more point to mention is that even more so than for buyer's or seller's lawyers, investment banker's lawyers do a brisk repeat business. Since transactions are an investment bank's bread and butter, they do them in huge volume. This is one of the reasons that many big New York firms prefer to focus their efforts on the less glamorous and exciting role of underwriter's counsel. While it may be less sexy work, the advantage is that your client is an entity that does deals almost constantly. In most cases the bankers and their counsel develop a good and smooth tempo as they do these deals; so much so that the interaction is much more like that of a business person and their in-house counsel.

4. Area Specialists

So far when I've referred to lawyers I've focused on corporate lawyers. But there are a myriad of related specialists that get called in on a deal. When a law firm is working on a Strategic Transaction you might view the corporate lawyer as the conductor of an orchestra. Following that analogy, the junior associates, paralegals and other support are the basic musicians, but occasionally a soloist is brought in. These are the specialists. They are often very senior and expert in their area, and while they have a limited role, it can often be critical. Here are some examples.

Intellectual Property

These lawyers ensure that the copyright, patent and trademark rights purported to be owned actually are. They advise on how to protect such rights and help file the necessary paperwork.

Tax

These lawyers advise on the tax implications of a deal and often help structure deals that are more tax efficient. Since a Strategic Transaction often triggers a tax event, these lawyers can play a crucial role and drive a substantial increase in the overall value of the deal through efficient tax structuring.

Litigation

These are the lawyers that advise on potential liabilities and lawsuits. They can help assess the risk of such events occurring and the chance of winning, and they are particularly relevant in industries where big liabilities abound (tobacco, healthcare and manufacturing might be good examples).

Trusts & Estates

Where individuals are involved, notably founders, these lawyers advise on how to structure a deal to maximize personal return, notably from a tax and estate tax point of view. Where a closely held company is being sold, this is likely to be a tremendously important issue if most of the stock is held by individuals who are about to recognize a massive personal gain on their investment.

Antitrust
In many situations, antitrust law may not be relevant to a deal, but where it is, it can entirely block a deal from happening. These lawyers understand the sometimes arcane and complex rules of U.S. – and where relevant, European Union – anti-trust law and how to determine if a violation may exist and also how to negotiate with the regulators concerning that determination.

Real Estate
Where land, leases or buildings are a material component of a deal these lawyers help understand the rights actually being acquired as well as the obligations.

All these specialists play a similar role in Strategic Transactions where relevant (i.e. where their topic is touched). They will be involved in due diligence, reviewing agreements, contracts and regulations in their area of specialty and helping the corporate lawyers present a complete picture to the client. They will help work with relevant regulators where necessary. They will help draft relevant sections of the documents, notably the representations and warranties sections.

There is often a bit of a love-hate relationship between these specialists and the corporate lawyers. As you might imagine, in most Strategic Transactions, the corporate lawyer is the center of attention and the work of the specialist is often fairly rote – reviewing due diligence and drafting a fairly standard representation section, but in some cases one or more specialist may become the center of a deal. For example, if anti-trust becomes a barrier to the completion of a deal, the anti-trust lawyer will become absolutely crucial and central. When purchasing a small technology company often intellectual property is the primary asset and therefore crucial. The challenge for the corporate lawyer is always to get sufficient focus from the sometimes bored specialist, and the challenge for the specialist is get the corporate lawyer to appreciate the importance of their particular piece of the puzzle.

9

The Investment Bankers

A.   Summary

Investment bankers are a powerful and often misunderstood player in Strategic Transactions. Before companies started employing in-house corporate development staff, they were essential experts who understood how to do a deal. But even with the emergence of in-house talent, investment bankers can play an important and valuable role. Most directly, they provide advisory services for a Strategic Transaction. These services can include expertise, market intelligence, process management, financial analysis, fairness opinions and sometimes just raw manpower. While investment bankers may not have as deep an understanding of the industry as their clients, they have extensive deal experience and strong financial skills that can be very valuable. Often they provide these services gratis well in advance of a deal, helping supplement a company's strategic planning and deal-sourcing efforts. Investment bankers also can be essential to funding a deal in their underwriting role, providing a unique access to public market financing sources. The analyst community embedded in investment banks also serves an important role, often affecting public market perception of a deal, and potentially the stock price of the companies involved.

ॐ ൽൽ ॐ

B. Investment Bankers: What's Their Role?

The role and importance of investment bankers have dramatically expanded since the early 1980s, as has their prestige and visibility in the popular culture. The movie "Wall Street" and the book Barbarians at the Gate were turning points where investment bankers, like the Wizard of Oz, emerged from behind the velvet curtain to reveal themselves as the driving force behind many of the "big deals" that we heard about. Investment bankers have developed a flashy powerful image as an elite corps of power brokers who drive deals, build companies and move financial markets. But beneath this veneer, they actually perform a set of fairly straightforward and obvious functions. It is crucial to understand the things that investment bankers actually do to make full use of their services and effectively hire, or negotiate with, one. Broadly speaking, you can divide the roles of investment bankers into two categories, underwriting and advisory.

The underwriting role is a direct result of the way our financial markets are structured and has become increasingly important as the amount of money invested by individuals directly in stocks or indirectly in mutual funds and pension funds increases and the amount of money placed in traditional savings accounts decreases. In the early 20th century, a much larger percentage of the money available to companies came from banks. Most people would put their money in banks who in turn would loan the money to companies. Very wealthy individuals would make equity investments directly into companies, which were thus owned by a small number of individuals. Today, the majority of most people's savings is not put into banks but instead invested in the capital markets either through direct ownership of stocks, or indirect ownership through mutual funds, pension funds and other vehicles. In turn, this money is made available to companies that either offer equity/stock or debt/bonds. The difference is that the number of individuals/entities that own this paper (the stocks or bonds) is several orders of magnitude larger than it was 100 years ago. In 1900, a company could get funding by going to a small number of individuals or entities (like banks) directly. In today's economy, most of the money available to companies (again particularly larger companies) requires marketing to thousands or even millions of individuals and entities. As a result, one of the primary roles of an investment bank is the underwriting, effectively the marketing and sale, of securities for issuing companies. For any company the most important underwriting is its first – the initial public offering of its stock or IPO. While it tends to be a higher profile and more scrutinized event (by the press, regulators and the market), it's basically the same exercise as any other offering except that the preparation work is much more extensive because less is known about the company and it doesn't yet have a track record as a public company.

In today's market, if a company wants to raise a material amount of capital (tens or hundreds of millions of dollars), the primary source will be the public markets and in almost all cases they will need to use an underwriter for this exercise. In simple terms, an underwriter reaches an agreement with a company to sell their offering of stock or bonds to the market of individual and institutional investors. The underwriter then uses its sales force of brokers to market the securities and develop a list of "indications of interest" from potential purchasers who are highly likely to purchase the securities when they are officially offered. The underwriter and seller then set an official offering date and sell the securities into the market. Because the company develops the selling document, called a prospectus, that the underwriter's sales force uses to sell the securities, the investment bank is taking the risk that if the facts on which it sold the securities (i.e. the information in the prospectus) is false, it can be subject to liability, just like the issuing company. Thus, when investment banks underwrite securities they will do extensive due diligence and a review of the issuing company to minimize that risk. Underwriting is a fairly straightforward business model; basically it serves as a seller or marketing agent. Investment bankers get paid for underwriting on a discount model. They get a pre-negotiated discount on every share they resell and while the discount will get smaller as the size of the deal gets larger, as a general matter, the larger the deal the more an investment bank will be paid. If the deal is particularly easy to place in the market, this can be a dramatic windfall for an investment bank.

The second important role that investment bankers play is that of advisor, and this will be our primary focus since it is here that investment bankers work closely with companies on Strategic Transactions. Unlike the underwriting role, here, the investment banker does not take a financial stake in a transaction or become a party to it. Instead, as the name suggests, the investment banker advises the client on the transaction and often acts as the client's representative. Mergers & Acquisitions is the highest profile investment bank advisory work but investment banks can advise on a very broad range of financial transactions. Basically, any transaction which involves some financial complexity or the need to identify a new partner company is a candidate for an investment bank as an advisor.

As an advisor in a Strategic Transaction an investment banker can play several roles, depending on the needs and sophistication of the client. We will discuss the various stages of a Strategic Transaction in more detail later in the book and the ways in which an investment banker can be involved in any or all of these stages. As a general matter, where a client chooses to take the lead, an investment banker will provide support, advice and manpower. Where the client lacks experience, expertise, or simply chooses to take a back seat, an investment banker will take the lead. For example, investment bankers can represent a client in negotiations or can simply provide a client with "color commentary" as the client negotiates. In some ways investment bankers are the utility players of Strategic Transactions and tend to fill whatever gaps are left in a team. But there are a couple of areas where investment bankers are especially expert.

1. Strategy and Target Identification

For large and well established clients or clients who hold the promise of a large lucrative deal (notably potential IPO candidates or ripe targets for acquisition), investment bankers will do a lot of up-front work to try and stimulate a deal. Investment bankers will often provide broad strategic advice and are particularly good at helping a company to understand a new market space and the players in it. It is important to note that even the most specialized industry-focused investment bankers will not know as much about an industry as the companies that operate in it. However, they have a broad basic knowledge of many industries, and a detailed knowledge of the financial, and notably the market, characteristics of these industries. Investment bankers can be very helpful when a company's management is trying to learn about a new industry or market sector, or when they are trying to understand financial market trends or the financials of competitors. For example, a transportation sector investment banker may not know as much about truck driver salaries as a United Parcel Service ("UPS") executive, but he may (a) be able to help the UPS executive understand more about a new industry space like internet email companies with which UPS competes or (b) give the UPS executive detailed information on trends of the stock trading for UPS and its competitors.

Once a company has decided to do a Strategic Transaction, bankers can be very helpful identifying potential companies (acquisition targets, buyers or partners) and gathering information about them. This is actually one thing that investment bankers do particularly well. They have the ability to marshal large amounts of information and data and have the "head count" to do so extremely quickly. They will often produce massive "pitch books" for their clients with detailed financial information, analysis and financial models on many potential transactions. In that sense, investment bankers are providing a very specialized kind of manpower.

2. Financial Analysis

Investment bankers are finance experts and one of their key roles is doing the complex financial analysis for a transaction. We will discuss valuation methods in more detail below, but in general terms you can think of this work like the old anti-drug commercial. In this commercial we see an egg and the voiceover says, "This is your brain." The egg is then cracked into a pan of hot oil and the voiceover says, "This is your brain on drugs." In the most general terms this is what investment bankers do for their clients. They show them the financial impact of a transaction on their company. "This is your company's financials today." "This is your company's financials after you do this deal." To be exact, the second phrase should read "This is your company's financials after you do this deal, if the information the other company has given us is accurate, and if your own projections of your company are accurate, and if our forecasts of the way your industry is growing are right, and if the integration plan you have works, and you realize all the synergies and benefits you predict, and if our predictions of the overall market and economy are not wrong." In fact, that is what they will say in the next item that investment bankers produce.

3. Fairness Opinions

In simplest terms, a fairness opinion is just that -- a written opinion by an investment banking firm stating that the financial terms of a deal are fair. In the case of a seller, the opinion is usually formally provided to the board of directors, but in many cases management is just as much of a client. In the case of a buyer while the opinion may be formally directed at the board, it is almost always management that is the real client.

The bankers can't speak to the due diligence that others have done, but they are the experts with regard to the purely financial terms and they can try to make a judgment as to whether the deal is fair and reasonable. But just as the client company has lawyers, so do the investment bankers, and this is where the fairness opinion gets complicated. Since a fairness opinion is a legal document prepared for a client, it creates the possibility of liability. In other words, if an investment banker takes the client's money and gives them a fairness opinion and the deal turns out to be a very bad one, the client can try to sue the investment banker. Not only could the client claim that they didn't get their money's worth from the investment banker and want the fee back, but worse they could claim that the "bad opinion" caused them to make a bad deal and they suffered huge damage that they want the investment banker to cover. Over time an investment bank writes dozens of such opinions and you could think of each one as a mine, a potential lawsuit, hanging over their heads. So the lawyers representing investment banks have crafted very extensive legal language, which you will find in any fairness opinion, designed to protect the investment bank from these lawsuits. The language is complex and detailed, but in short it generally says that this opinion is based on a large number of items and that if any of these are not accurate, the opinion cannot be relied upon. These items include all the financial information provided to the investment bank by both the buyer and the seller, the due diligence information provided to the investment bank and provided to other parties like the lawyers and accountants, any market information provided to the investment bank by any party, and so on. The fairness opinion also makes it clear that the opinion is based only on the investment banks best guess on a variety of matters that are out of its control including market conditions, interest rates and overall economic trends.

In net, the result is a document that many people would say is weak at best. A fairness opinion "is not a guarantee of the fairness of a transaction, and even more, it is not a guarantee that no better offer can be found. It is just an informed opinion regarding the proposed transaction as presented to the financial advisor."[36] The only real liability an investment bank has for its fairness opinions are if the bank "negligently or willfully issues an incorrect opinion."[37] So while the fairness opinion says the deal is fair, don't expect to get any satisfaction from the investment bank if it turns out to be wrong, unless they have been exceedingly negligent, or actually fraudulent, in preparing it, which is a high standard to meet. While investment banks are occasionally named in shareholder lawsuits after public acquisitions, they are very rarely held liable based on a fairness opinion they've written. In the rare cases where the bank doesn't feel able to write a positive fairness opinion, they will usually quietly and discretely resign from the transaction, making it unlikely that shareholders will ever hear about it.[38] In these situations the client company is usually able to find another, perhaps smaller or more risk-tolerant, investment bank that is willing to issue the fairness opinion.

---

[36] Roberts, Todd, "Financial Advisors and Fairness Opinions in Corporate Control Transactions," directorship, Vol. 27 Issue 9, October 2001, p14, p3.
[37] Roberts, Todd, "Financial Advisors and Fairness Opinions in Corporate Control Transactions," directorship, Vol. 27 Issue 9, October 2001, p14, p3.
[38] Sweeney, Paul, "Who Says It's a Fair Deal," Journal of Accountancy, Vol. 188 Issue 2, August 1999, p44.

So why do people still use fairness opinions if they're the legal equivalent of Swiss cheese. In point of fact, many people don't. Outside the United States fairness opinions are rarely seen and I've found that large European companies generally find the notion of a fairness opinion to be a somewhat humorous American quirk. Even in the United States the use of the fairness opinion is on the decline. But fairness opinions are still widely used, particularly in large deals.[39] One reason is that investment banks still sell them. In an age where investment banking services are effectively, if not formally, bundled together, the fairness opinion may be the "floor mats and undercoating" of financial services; something offered and purchased as an afterthought at the end of a list of more crucial services like M&A advisory and underwriting. Another possibility is the classic "CYA" ("cover your ass" for the less earthy readers among you). A board of directors is highly sensitive to the potential of being sued and Strategic Transactions are like magnets for lawsuits since they involve dramatic changes in the strategy, finances and fate of a company. The small incremental cost of a fairness opinion will seem well worth it to a board if only to provide evidence that they tried to ensure that the deal was in the best interests of the shareholders. Finally, one might argue that forcing an investment bank to "put its money where its mouth is" at least to the extent of a signed document (though of dubious legal value) might ensure a certain level of focus and effort by senior bankers to ensure accurate and diligent efforts. If you're a small company using a very large and powerful investment bank, the fear of getting lost in the shuffle and handed off to a junior and inexperienced banker is very real. To some extent a fairness opinion may keep the senior bankers involved, at least on the periphery, in a deal that while incredibly important to you, may be a very small matter financially to them.

In the final analysis, I think fairness opinions are of modest value. They provide an illusory legal recourse to investment bankers that you'll almost

---

[39] Between 1990-2001, over two thousand fairness opinions were issued. But the number of fairness opinions has declined substantially from over 450 in 1997 to just over 211 in 2001. Hunt, Peter, Structuring Mergers & Acquisitions, (Aspen 2003).

never succeed in enforcing. They give a board of directors and management a sense of CYA (aka "cover your ass") better achieved through greater involvement in the deal and careful interrogation of the team leading it. To the extent that you need the fear of legal liability to motivate senior focus by your investment bank, it may be better to go with a different bank. Having said that, in the grand scheme of a Strategic Transaction the cost of a fairness opinion is fairly low. In a billion dollar deal the fairness opinion may cost you a few million more, representing a few dozen basis points. Thus, while it may have little value, it also isn't a huge burden.

4. Process Management

Launching a Strategic Transaction is a lot like putting on a play. There is a lot going on both in front and behind the curtain and it all has to be coordinated. We will talk more about all the internal resources that have to be mustered inside the buyer and the seller, but even the coordination with other entities is daunting. Each side will have their own set of advisors and many actions need to be coordinated. If the process chosen involves multiple buyers, the process is exponentially more complicated. Investment bankers have a great deal of expertise in managing these processes. Perhaps more importantly, investment banks are built to handle the massive peaks of manpower and activity that occur in Strategic Transactions. Whether it's the need to develop a complex financial model overnight, or coordinating a 30-way conference call with associated material, investment banks are custom built for process management. When you hire an investment bank, part of what you're buying is access to an infrastructure that usually includes round the clock document processing and duplicating, global offices with conference facilities in dozens of cities, complex telecommunications setups, and a large pool of highly trained professionals that can be brought in for peak work. It is not unusual for an investment bank to field a team of twenty or thirty extra professionals (beyond the team already dedicated to the transaction) to handle a peak period such as the collection and analysis of bids or an IPO road show. Even for a client who is highly sophisticated, this is a capability that cannot be efficiently duplicated. This in part may explain why even the most sophisticated companies still use investment bank advisors on their larger and more complex deals.

C. Investment Bankers: The People and What They Do

It is important to set the stage by describing the fairly hierarchical and ordered organizational structure of an investment bank. Within each group, there are a number of different "levels" of investment banker. We begin with analysts. Not to be too harsh but analysts are generally the "cannon fodder" of an investment banking team (note here I'm not talking about research analysts which will be covered shortly). Analysts are generally hired directly out of top colleges and usually only stay with a bank two to three years. They are responsible for building large and complex financial models and doing a variety of other "scut work" including developing presentation material, organizing meetings and doing financial research. They tend to be highly motivated and exceedingly bright young people who are willing to work egregious hours (typically 70 to 90 per week – I'm not kidding!) for a jump-start to their young careers. In exchange for the long hours and great stress, they get a fantastic resume foundation since most people in the industry know that an analyst program is a stellar training exercise. They also get relatively exciting roles with a relatively high level of responsibility for their age, and while they are by far the cheapest members of the team, with compensation in the mid to high five figures, this is still by far the best paying job for kids straight out of college.

Next up the ladder are associates. Between analysts and associates is the gap of business school and often some other work experience. While in rare cases analysts are promoted directly to associate, the vast majority of associates are hired out of top business schools. Rather than viewing this as a short-term experience, an associate views this as the start of their career. An associate's life is arguably even tougher than that of an analyst. Early on they tend to work the same hours and have the added pressure of management and the stress of knowing that their performance impacts a much longer potential career in the firm. In addition to managing analysts and reviewing their work, associates typically do a lot of work on presentation material and in a live deal do a lot of process management. Their compensation is a leap above analysts, with base salary usually around 100,000 and a first full year bonus well into the six figures.

After three to four years as an associate, bankers are promoted to vice president. While promotion is not guaranteed, in a good economy most associates will usually make the jump. Note here the difference between corporate and investment banking titles. In most corporations, vice president is a fairly senior role. One example I like is that of a particular vice president at General Motors who was in charge of all their Brazil operations, which had tens of thousands of employees. By contrast, at an investment bank, a vice president is usually a smart post-MBA in their late twenties or early thirties who usually manages a team of two to five analysts. In addition to managing associates and analysts, vice presidents take a more direct role with clients, spending a lot of their time formulating potential pitches to clients and in many cases either leading or taking part in those presentations. They also usually have responsibility for running all but the largest live deals.

Next up are directors. By the time you reach director, you are in full client development mode and this is your opportunity to show the firm that you can build a book of business. Directors are in many senses auditioning for a managing director role and are largely focused on building a practice. At this point they are often the senior-most banker focused on a mid-sized client. Finally, there are managing directors. These are the senior-most investment bankers, who are almost exclusively focused on client development for the largest and most important clients, with some time set aside for management roles. Some managing directors become more traditional senior managers, running a group or even the entire investment banking operations. Other managing directors prefer to remain primarily in a sales role, eschewing management responsibilities to build a large business and portfolio of clients.

D. Investment Bankers: Economic Model and Their Incentives/Biases

In many ways, the investment bank economic model is the exact opposite of the lawyer model. For an advisory assignment, the standard terms provide a very large success fee only payable if the deal is closed. The success fee is based on the size of the deal, and most banks have a standard sliding scale they use to determine the fee. In many cases, particularly for good or large clients, banks will discount from the standard scale, but still get paid on a percentage basis, and the numbers can be huge. Fee schedules will vary from firm to firm and definitely vary based on the strength of the market. In recent years with the Strategic Transaction market particularly weak, many investment banks have been dramatically discounting their fees. By contrast, in the late 1990s when investment bankers were in high demand, many banks were able to charge premium rates. Here's one example of a standard pricing model that an investment bank might use on an advisory assignment:

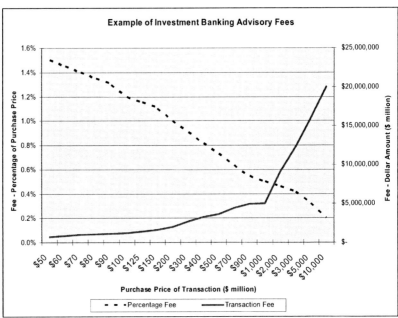

While basic out of pocket expenses are sometimes covered, the cost of working on an advisory assignment that doesn't end in a deal is substantial for the investment bank. Investment banks have a dramatic financial incentive to get a deal closed, and the only force that moderates this incentive, is the notion that they will have a repeated and regular relationship with the client which is in jeopardy if they push for a very bad deal to get done. It is generally accepted that investment bankers will always be biased toward a deal. In some ways they are seen as an advocate of the deal as much, or more than, as an advocate of their client.

The same deal-closing incentives drive individual banker's incentives by the time they are a few years into their careers. Even at a junior level, individual investment bankers' compensation is heavily bonus driven. Investment bankers get a base salary and an annual bonus, paid in cash (with an equity component at the more senior levels). Unlike most industries, the bonus makes up a majority of most investment bankers' compensation and is highly volatile and uncertain. Each year investment bankers eagerly await bonus season and watch with anticipation to see what they and their competitor firms' employees get paid. In a typical year, a mid-level investment banker might make a base salary of $100,000 with a bonus of perhaps $300,000. That same banker could bring home only $100,000 in bonus in a weak year and perhaps $500,000 in a very strong year. While salaries vary dramatically year to year, it's safe to assume that in a normalized market, an associate will bring home $150,000 - $400,000, a vice president will bring home $300,000 - $700,000, a director will bring home $500,000 - $1,000,000 and a managing director will make at least $1,000,000 and up to $10,000,000, in all but the most extreme markets. Both the size of these numbers and the range should demonstrate the importance of performance, and that is measured most clearly by deals closed and revenue brought in to the firm.

Bonuses may not be directly tied to deals closed at a junior level, but even at the associate level, being associated with a successful deal can have an indirect impact on your bonus. By the time an investment banker reaches senior vice president level and certainly when they reach the director title, their compensation is closely related to the business they bring in. At the more senior managing director level, compensation is almost always tied directly to transactions done and revenue generated. Thus, a managing director who does a lot of deals can make an order of magnitude more than another managing director who has had modest success bringing in deals. Things are a little more complex for investment bankers that are not direct "relationship managers" and don't own the direct client relationship. Some specialists don't have this direct selling role, but are brought in on a deal as area experts. Even these bankers, however, get paid in large part based on the revenue they help bring into the firm. Though there are several other variations and exceptions including compensation for a management role and for being associated with or working on another banker's live deal, as a general matter, the key to success and compensation as an investment banker, as is true for the organization itself, is bringing in and closing deals.

E. Management of, or Interaction with, Investment Bankers

The key question for management to ask, and to ask very early in the process, is whether an investment bank is needed as an advisor at all. In many cases, a company may not need an investment bank advisor or may only need one in a very limited role, if its own management team and corporate development team has sufficient expertise. There is clearly a trend to bring the expertise to do deals in-house and today many companies either don't use investment bankers as deal advisors, or only use them for the largest deals.

At the end of the day there are many reasons that one might want to retain an investment bank advisor for a Strategic Transaction. In most cases the investment bank will have worked with the company for months or even years before the deal is launched and there may well be a feeling of obligation, beyond any specific need for advice. More than most other players in a Strategic Transaction, investment bankers often get a seat at the table – a role in the transaction – as a result of a personal relationship developed over time with the CFO or CEO of the client. Investment bankers can also bring some unique value to a deal. In a situation where the long-term fate of the company hangs in the balance, many CEOs will err on the side of caution and use the belt and suspenders approach of hiring an investment bank, even if there is not specific clear need. As we've discussed, while Fairness Opinions may not really give much recourse against the investment bank, they do give management and the board some comfort that the terms of the deal are reasonable.

Investment bankers are also often hired as a reward for work done in the past. For every deal that actually gets done, dozens are considered. Investment bankers not only have access to data and industry insights, but also a large pool of professional resources. As a result, one of the informal services that investment bankers provide to clients and potential clients is a stream of gratis work. This can take the form of "pitches" that are made to a company proposing potential deals. It can be more explicit in the form of a project that the company asks the banker to do. In any case, investment bankers will often invest hundreds if not thousands of man-hours into free work for clients in anticipation of getting retained on a deal. When you start to think that bankers are overpaid for a simple advisory project it's good to remember that the banker may have spent the prior two years doing a steady stream of free work for the client.

While in theory you might hire an investment banker to advise on any transaction, their strength is really in acquisitions, divestitures and sometimes equity investments. This is because they excel at doing the complex financial analysis of such deals. But they are not particularly strong at business strategy and while the industry specialists know enough about their sector and clients' business to advise them on large deals, they don't know as much as their clients, or industry specialty consultants, about the core operations of the business.

I should note the interaction between hiring investment bankers as advisors and as underwriters. In most cases, a company has a lot more leeway in choosing an advisor. Many banks, both small and large, can provide good advisory services. But, if a company wants to place a large amount of securities, there are only a handful of large firms with the brokerage network and institutional sales force to be the lead underwriter. Thus, you will often see companies choose advisors on the basis of who they want to help them place a related offering.

Finally, it is important when dealing with investment bankers to remember that their fundamental economic model gives them a powerful bias towards doing deals. Whether it's an advisory assignment or underwriting an offering, investment banks only get paid when the deal is done, but then get paid royally. This is not a criticism of investment bankers, but simply recognition of the way their business works.

F. Variations

1. Industry Specialists/Relationship Managers

Most investment banks take an industry-segmented approach to building relationships with their client companies. Therefore, they break their investment bankers into industry groups, and provide some product specialists for products that are particularly complex. Different banks provide different levels of granularity for their industry groups, and different industries require different levels of granularity. During the peak of the Internet boom it was not unusual to see banks sub-segment their technology teams into groups like Internet Retail and Infrastructure Software. The premise of this structure is that companies want to deal with bankers that first and foremost understand their business and sector. Thus, the banker who has primary responsibility for a company is usually a specialist in the company's sector. These bankers are called "relationship managers" and are supposed to be the primary point of contact between the company and the investment bank for all its services. In Strategic Transactions, knowledge of the company, its business and the sector is particularly important if the banker is to provide valuable help identifying potential counterparties, advising on valuation and important terms, and offering a network of helpful contacts and introductions.

Some investment banks choose to build a specialty group focused entirely on relationship management. Goldman Sachs has such a group.[40] These relationship managers may have some industry expertise, but they are first and foremost conduits through which a client can access the various services of the firm, and, more importantly, through which the firm can market its full range of products and services to large and complex clients. These relationship managers focus their attentions on the largest multinational corporate clients, who are most likely to require highly focused attention and time commitment and are likely to be potential clients for a wide range of the firm's services. These are companies like IBM, Microsoft or General Electric.

2. Product Specialists

There are product specialists who have deep expertise in a particular financial product. Generally these are products so complex or specialized that they require such expertise. The best examples might be high yield debt (with its myriad of complex covenants and legal documentation) or mergers & acquisitions. In each case, the bankers who work in these areas will generally not be the key relationship contact with the client, but will be brought in as a specialist. One exception to this rule will be found with firms that do certain kinds of deals so frequently that they develop a close relationship with the specialist. Sometimes this relationship can even eclipse the connection to the "relationship manager" who is covering them. A good example of this would be Tyco or Cisco. These companies did so many

[40] "Goldman Sachs' Global Relationship Management team (GRM) brings together two of our most deeply held principles: client focus and teamwork. Their mandate is to think broadly and strategically about the financial alternatives for our clients. In effect, GRM is at the intersection of our clients' needs and Goldman Sachs' capabilities. Teamwork and client focus come together in GRM to create a level of service to our clients that can be identified as uniquely Goldman Sachs." See www.gs.com/our_firm/investor_relations/financial_reports/annual_reports/2002/client/grm.html

Strategic Transactions that I suspect that their closest point of contact in an investment bank would not be the banker covering their industry sector but rather the M&A specialist. Certainly this could be true of Tyco in particular, as it is spread across so many industry sectors.

For Strategic Transactions, the most relevant group of specialists is the M&A bankers. They are less likely to be called in if the deal is small and/or "plain vanilla," meaning that it is fairly straightforward and does not have unusual or complex features. Complexities that might call for an M&A banker's expertise would include hostile deals, complex auction processes, difficult valuation exercises or complex payment terms.

While almost all investment banks still have product specialists, many of these specialists also have industry expertise to make them more valuable to their clients. Thus, some High Yield bankers may specialize in Telecommunications deals, and some M&A bankers may specialize in Media. There is always a vague line between product specialists with some industry knowledge and industry specialists with some product knowledge.

3. Financing Bankers

Though we're focused here on Strategic Transactions, it's important to remember that a big part of what investment banking firms do is underwrite securities. Sometimes a client is just raising capital for general operations and sometimes specifically to fund a Strategic Transaction. In either case, a major role of the investment bank is to sell those securities. The bankers who take the lead in actually getting the securities into the market are the sales & trading bankers who sit on sales desks. They are responsible for selling securities of their investment banking colleague's clients, to the investment bank's trading customers (either institutional investors or individual investors through the firm's brokerage network). They may also trade for the firm's own account. Like the product specialists, while trading bankers may not be the primary point of contact with the client company, if the client does deals on a regular basis they may have a strong relationship with them. For a company like General Motors or Capital One that at some points issues equity or debt securities on a quarterly or even monthly basis, there is likely to be a strong direct relationship between the bankers on the trading desk and the finance executives of the company.

4. Research Analysts

Research analysts present the most glaring exception to the general title structure (discussed above) in investment banks. The research division of an investment bank is theoretically walled off from the investment bankers. Research is responsible for putting out, again theoretically, unbiased analysis of companies they choose to cover. The title Research Analyst is generally used for a broad range of people in this group, from the more junior analysts up to the senior ones in charge of covering the largest companies. While there may be internal titles like vice president and managing director, these people are all usually referred to by outside entities as simply research analysts. Thus, in order to understand how senior or junior, and therefore how well paid a research analyst is, the best measure is to look at what they cover. The most junior research analysts function like investment banking analysts and associates, assisting other research analysts and don't have their names on any reports. More senior research analysts may cover the smaller companies in their sector or share credit for reports on larger companies with their boss. These are more akin to vice presidents or directors. Finally, the most senior research analysts will cover the largest companies and likely have overall responsibility for their sector. These are really akin to managing directors. Research analysts generally get paid somewhat less than their corresponding level in investment banking but not much less, and arguably have a slightly better lifestyle and hours, but again not much better. They tend to be somewhat more analytical and intellectual than their counterparts in investment banking and though like everyone at an investment bank they are somewhat involved in the sales process, it is much less central to their jobs than for investment bankers.

In years past, investment banks would also offer the chance to have their research analyst cover a stock if they were chosen for an offering. Or if the company was already covered by the analyst, they might offer the opportunity to explain the deal to the analyst, hopefully increasing the possibility that the analyst would look kindly on the deal when it was announced. But in wake of a wave of scandals over research analysts hyping stocks based on investment banking relationships, the wall has come down hard on these cross promotions. In today's environment, investment bankers are barred from offering any such quid pro quos and for the most part research analysts are fairly independent of the investment banking relationships of their firms.

One final point should be made about the various players that a buyer or seller might hire in a deal. Early in my career as a lawyer I was advising a client on a $600 million offering of high yield bonds. The legal team worked for months to prepare the deal documentation and built up a bill of over $1 million, but as we sat at the financial printer putting the final numbers into the prospectus, including the investment banker discount which must be disclosed, I realized that the bankers, who had been able to easily place these bonds in a matter of days during a particularly good market, were netting over $60 million for their work. This is an important contrast point between the way investment bankers and other service providers, like lawyers, work and are compensated. Investment bankers are paid extremely high fees but only when a deal happens. They expend substantial effort cultivating relationships with clients and working with them on potential deals but only get paid if the deal closes, but when it happens, they get paid well. By contrast, lawyers, accountants and other service providers generally get paid on an hourly or project basis, at much lower total fee levels, but they get paid whether the deal happens or not. One insight that we gain from this is that while most service providers have a somewhat unbiased view on the outcome of a deal, investment bankers have a powerful incentive to make the deal happen. So when you are getting advice from an investment banker or any other advisor paid on a "success basis," you must remember the adverse incentive at work.

10

The Other Advisors

A. Consultants/Auditors

Consulting and auditing is a massive industry and encompasses a wide range of services from high level management consulting from such firms as McKinsey, to systems integration and more technical consulting provided by IBM, to a myriad of small consulting firms with a variety of specialties. Then there are the "big few" auditing and accounting firms, and many smaller ones, that perform financial audits and often also have consulting arms. Consultants and auditors can become involved in almost every aspect of the operation of a business, but for purposes of this book we will only focus on their relatively limited direct role in Strategic Transactions.

In general, there are four key areas where consultants are likely to have the largest impact on a Strategic Transaction: strategy development, due diligence, integration planning and integration execution. In each area they will usually support and supplement the work of the line management team. As long-term advisors they will sometimes have a broad counseling role, and there are certainly some specialist consulting firms that try to delve deeper into the Strategic Transaction process, but as a general matter these are the roles in which you are most likely to see consultants.

Strategy development is the area that is most likely to be driven by consultants. Companies often find themselves stagnating, and need to "think out of the box." By definition, company management are the experts in their existing business, and so it is when they are considering a departure from standard operation that they are likely to seek outside advice. Consultants are often brought in to lead, drive and contribute to a formal strategic planning process. In addition to the substantive insights that they may provide, consultants help structure and drive the process of strategic discovery. Some would argue that they also provide executive management with cover (in a similar manner to the cover that fairness opinions can provide to the board) to make a dramatic change in the operation or direction of the company. Consultants are often key players in a corporate strategy process that ends up driving a Strategic Transaction.

໙ ೞ๛ ೞ

Once a deal is underway, consultants may often have a role in due diligence. Consultants tend to have greater industry and operational expertise than either lawyers or investment bankers so if a line management team simply needs additional bodies to conduct due diligence, they may call on a consulting firm. Consultants with a particular specialty may also be used in due diligence. For example, there are environmental consultants that are often used to assess potential environmental liabilities on industrial manufacturing properties that are part of an acquisition.

Integration planning is also an area where consultants can contribute. Since, again unlike other outside advisors, they understand operational aspects of the business they are well equipped to help the line management team plan for the integration of operations, staff, systems, products and brands. Consultants also bring some objectivity to the exercise. Integrating a business or partnership can have dramatic ramifications for people within the relevant business. If a manager is afraid for her job or just worried about her career, she may not make decisions that are in the best interest of the company. For example, a manager who sees an intimidating counterpart in the other organization may be tempted to try and press for their elimination. Consultants are outsiders who can objectively help line management make the best choices for the company.

Some consulting firms have a hybrid role that involves some of the work traditionally performed by investment banks. Consulting firms, particularly those with historical roots in accounting and auditing, will often offer valuation services and some are even pushing into full investment banking advisory services. Firms like KPMG have a fairly extensive Strategic Transaction advisory offering. For companies that don't need the underwriting firepower of an investment bank, consulting firms may present a lower cost alternative that provides the same quality of analysis. These firms have already started to cut into investment bank business on the advisory side and I'd suspect that this trend will continue, with the consulting/auditing firms now offering a "one stop shop" for strategic consulting, audit, due diligence, valuation and Strategic Transaction advisory services. While historically they've nipped at the heels of the investment banks, making greater headway in the small and mid-cap market, I'd expect them to push further into the bread and butter Fortune 1000 space over time.

Auditors have a smaller, and more well-defined, set of roles in a Strategic Transaction. Any public company and most significant-sized private companies already have an auditor for their financials. In the case of a smaller company that does not have audited financials, a buyer will often require an audit be done. In any case, a buyer will likely bring in their own auditors to review the financials and audits of a target company. Even if a company is public and has public audited financials, an acquirer may want their own auditors to review the financials and in particular make sure that there are no differences between the ways the two companies account for things. If you recall the "this is your brain and this is your brain on drugs" analogy, one of the keys to financial pro forma is to make sure that you are comparing "apples to apples" and using the same accounting rules for both companies. When a target doesn't have audited financials, the role of an auditor in due diligence is even more crucial. They must not only review accounting procedures but the underlying numbers themselves.

B. Public Relations/Communications Firm

Public relations firms are used today by almost every company. Whether they're working on broad-based branding initiatives, or specific product launches, or controversial topics like lawsuits or government lobbying, public relations firms tend to be involved in many major issues for big and even mid-sized companies. Strategic Transactions are no different. When a company does a deal, they are worried about how it will be perceived by a variety of groups including shareholders, employees, customers, competitors and regulators. Internal public relations staff as well as an outside public relations firm may be involved in helping to craft the message and will certainly be used to get the message out. In many deals this role can be limited to just working with the corporate development staff to draft a short press release and then sending it out. For larger and more controversial deals, a public relations firm might work on crafting a variety of messages to different constituencies and pro-actively seeking out the press to get the message out. For example, when Daimler and Chrysler were merging I'm certain that Chrysler's public relations staff and firms were actively involved in getting out the message to the public and to regulators that would have to approve the deal that it wouldn't lead to massive U.S. layoffs. Similarly, they were certainly involved in putting out a message to Chrysler shareholders that this was a good deal for them.

When a deal is higher profile, public relations staff will have to work with the deal team to be armed with detailed information about the nature and benefits of the deal since they can expect to get peppered with questions from the press. They usually get briefed and prepare standard questions and answers they expect to get.

While you might think that putting a spin on a deal is just window dressing, for a public company, or one in a heavily regulated space, the damage done by not getting out a good story is dramatic and very real. If a public company announces a deal that is not well received, in part determined by how it's reported, the stock price can drop precipitously and sometimes never fully recovers. Similarly, a bad spin on a deal can spur regulators to action and sometimes this leads to the deal being entirely blocked. A good public relations spin may not change the long-term outcome of a deal, but it can create short-term benefits and avoid short-term damage. At the very least, it may deliver the benefit of the doubt from investors and give the company time to prove their thesis that the deal was in the best interests of the shareholders.

C. Proxy/Shareholder Services Firm

I won't spend much time on proxy firms but it's useful to understand their basic role. Whenever a public company does a deal that is sufficiently large and material, they may need to seek shareholder approval. Without getting into the legal complexities of when shareholder approval is needed, it's safe to say that many sales of companies, mergers of equals or even an acquisition of another company that is almost the same size, will require a shareholder vote. Of course, any time one party launches a hostile transaction a shareholder vote will almost certainly be required to overturn the rejection of the target company board. In these situations, companies hire firms that help them get their message to the shareholders and lobby shareholders to support the transaction. In the case of a hostile offer, both sides may utilize these services. While it's a relatively rare occurrence, when it happens the stakes are high indeed.

D. Financial Printers

In the days before desktop publishing and the Internet, if you wanted to create high quality bound documents like annual reports, other shareholder communications and filings with the SEC, you needed a big physical plant. No company was justified in spending the money to build such a facility for their own internal documentation, so financial printers emerged to service this need. These firms are often subsidiaries of bigger publishing houses but specialize in printing financial documents that require an extremely high level of service and speed. They offer clients an ability to do real-time editing of the document and then print thousands of copies in a matter of hours. The fees are extremely high, but they are inconsequential in the context of a transaction or company. For example, a company might spend $200,000 to print a prospectus on a $100 million offering. In the last decade, new technologies have made many of the financial printers' services obsolete. The SEC now accepts filings electronically through a system called EDGAR and hundreds of law firms have the facilities to make those filings directly. Companies still go to financial printers to do the actual printing of large volume documents like annual reports and prospectuses, but they do far more of the word processing in-house or at their lawyers' offices, substantially reducing the fees to financial printers.[41]

---

[41] In some ways, financial printers may eventually become the buggy-whip manufacturers of our time. While they may not become entirely extinct, their heyday has clearly passed. As more and more is done electronically and online, the need for huge numbers of glossy copies of documents may disappear. It's probably years away from happening but at some point I'd suspect that most shareholder communications like annual reports and offering documents will be transmitted electronically. At that point financial printers' role will be extremely small.

11

The Regulators and the Press

A. Regulators

There is a huge literature discussing government regulation of deals and companies in detail, and this is of course the area where lawyers are most valuable and essential. While you need to leave the details of compliance and detailed regulation to your legal counsel, it's important to have a general idea of how, and by whom, a company is regulated.

Every company is regulated by the state in which it is headquartered, the federal government and, to a lesser but significant extent, the states, towns and counties where it has operations. Among the federal and state regulations governing a company are those concerning ownership structure and protection of investors. Private companies are subject to some such obligations but the bar is dramatically raised when a company is publicly held. This is since the government is much more concerned with protecting small public investors. When a company is public, it is subject to a myriad of federal and state regulations as well as the rules of the exchange on which its securities are traded. This section provides a brief discussion of the major areas of regulation in the United States.[42]

∂ ⬥ ◈

---

[42] While there are similar structures in other countries, there are also significant differences in how European and Asian companies are regulated and by whom.

1. Securities and Exchange Commission

The Securities and Exchange Commission (the "SEC") is the federal agency responsible for regulating publicly traded and owned companies and funds. Its authority is primarily based on the Securities Act of 1933 and the Exchange Act of 1934, as well as the 1940 Act governing mutual funds. These were enacted in the wake of the 1929 crash and were driven by a perceived need to protect smaller individual investors. Therefore, the driving force behind most parts of these regulations is the need to provide smaller individual investors (notably the proverbial "widows and orphans") with full information, and protection. The premise is that larger professional investors are generally in need of less protection and thus, the biggest exemptions to these Acts are for entities that can demonstrate that their only investors are a small population of large, sophisticated parties, which are presumed to be able to take care of themselves and require far less protection from federal regulators.

The 1933 and 1934 Acts, as they are known, have two primary types of regulation. They bar certain behavior, and they require certain disclosure and information be provided to investors. The idea is to set a minimum standard of behavior for any public company or fund, and then beyond that ensure that the investors are fully informed about the risks and actions of the company or fund. The SEC is therefore heavily involved in overseeing the activities of publicly held companies and funds, but relatively unobtrusive when it comes to privately held companies.

2. State and Local Regulators

Any U.S. company must be formally incorporated in a particular state and is subject to that state's corporate law, in addition to federal regulations like the ones enforced by the SEC. Different states can have substantially different levels of regulation, and taxation, of corporations. Similarly, since the corporations are most readily subject to litigation in that states' court system, choice of where to incorporate may depend on how friendly and easy to deal with the state courts are. For a variety of reasons, Delaware has become a de facto state of incorporation for many companies, but many other companies, particularly those with political ties to a particular state, are incorporated in states other than Delaware. Until recently, the states were not particularly aggressive regulators of companies, leaving it to federal regulators and the court system to monitor the activities even of companies incorporated in their state. In the wake of Enron, WorldCom and the controversy over Wall Street research analysts' roles in touting technology stocks, a variety of state attorneys general have become more activist in prosecuting companies for violations of their state corporate law, and they have not limited their actions to companies incorporated in their states. Two particular examples are the work of Elliot Spitzer, the attorney general of New York State, investigating and ultimately negotiating a settlement with investment banks on Wall Street regarding research analyst recommendations for technology stocks, and charges filed by W. A. Drew Edmondson, the Attorney General of Oklahoma, in August of 2003 against WorldCom and some of its former executives, for violations of Oklahoma securities laws. Whether they aim to fill a gap left by perceived weak federal enforcement, or simply seek to seize on a high profile and publicly popular cause, it seems that state regulators are likely to become more involved in oversight and prosecution of corporations.

Local regulators are usually the most passive. In most cases a locality is overjoyed to have a company located there, employing its residents. However, on occasion localities can become more aggressive enforcing local regulations. I found one comical example of this when I was negotiating to purchase a company whose headquarters was in the center of the historic downtown district of one mid-sized southern city. The company had bought a local landmark called the Commerce Building and in the spirit of the technology boom had added an "e" to the sign on the façade, renaming it the eCommerce building. As we prepared to close the deal our lawyers discovered that this action had technically violated the town ordinances on preservation of historical landmarks and we had to ask the seller to get an exemption from the local government. The prospect of pleasing a major future employer was more than enough to induce the local government to grant the exemption, and we were soon the proud owners of the eCommerce Building.

3. Industry Regulators

There are numerous federal and state regulatory bodies that focus on particular industries or activities. From local liquor licenses to the Environmental Protection Agency (EPA), various agencies oversee the activities of companies, and the level of regulation and scrutiny vary widely. When a Strategic Transaction brings a company into a new business or sector it's important for them to understand the regulatory schema that covers that business. In some cases a lot of additional work and effort will be required to comply with the new regulations. For example, a restaurant that starts serving liquor will suddenly be subject to substantial additional and different regulation. On a larger scale, when a company chooses to become a bank, or a telecommunications carrier, or television broadcaster, they are subject to a new regulatory schema, often at both federal and state levels. In some cases, the industry regulators approval will actually be required to complete a Strategic Transaction, particularly when it brings a new player into a regulated business.

4. Foreign Regulators

While the differences between state regulations are generally not huge, moving across national borders can trigger substantial regulatory issues. When undertaking any cross-border Strategic Transaction you have to consider carefully the regulatory environment of both companies and recognize that different countries can have a substantially different take on basic regulatory structures like anti-trust law. Domestic ownership requirements are one particular area where cross-border transactions differ from domestic ones. Almost every country has some industries or businesses where there are minimum levels of domestic ownership required. Even in the United States, such limits exist for ownership of media outlets like television and radio stations, and in some countries like China, most businesses are subject to a requirement that a substantial minority, or even a majority, of ownership stays in the hands of citizens of that country. There are also big differences in basic regulatory structures that affect nearly all companies, like environmental standards and labor issues. For example, in many European countries there are strict limits on how and when employees can be laid off. Before doing a deal with a company in these countries that involves synergies through redundancy it would be wise to make sure that you will be allowed to take advantage of these synergies and not required to continue employing redundant staff.

5. *Department of Justice/Federal Trade Commission*

The United States was a pioneer in the development of anti-trust or competition law, but today many other countries, notably the European Union, have strong anti-trust regimes as well. In the United States, the Department of Justice and the Federal Trade Commission share responsibility for enforcing these regulations. The basic premise of anti-trust law is that companies are not allowed to compete unfairly, but the question of when competition is unfair is exceedingly complex. There are a variety of measures and metrics, both qualitative and quantitative, used to determine when a company is competing unfairly. As a general matter, any company that has substantial power over the market and pricing for a product, either through large market share or control of one stage of the market-like distribution or supply of raw material, and uses such power to its advantage, is at least potentially in danger of being deemed to be violating anti-trust laws. Where one draws the lines to define a market, a product or a sector is uncertain and can make the difference in such a determination. If an anti-trust violation is found or alleged in a deal, there may be a way to appease the regulators through a change to the deal structure such as carving out a piece of the assets or operations to be acquired, or committing to divest other assets. At a minimum, an anti-trust issue will substantially slow and complicate a deal and often block it entirely.

There is a huge literature, and an entire legal specialty, devoted to drawing those lines and determining where anti-trust violations exist, which I won't attempt to summarize, but I can make a general observation. In any situation where a company's market share, geographical coverage, position along the supply chain, or product range, are being materially expanded, you need to at least consider the potential for anti-trust action by the regulators. Strategic Transactions often cause such a sudden shift in these and other metrics. Therefore, in any Strategic Transaction it is worthwhile to at least ask the question of whether an anti-trust issue will be raised.

In summary, when considering a Strategic Transaction it is important to consider whether any regulator will have a role or interest. Regulators may be involved because of the nature of the transaction or the nature of the parties. The counterparty may be subject to regulations and the oversight of regulators with whom you are not familiar. When entering a new business, particularly through a Strategic Transaction, you need to be sure to understand the regulatory framework that you are entering. Like any other cost or requirement of a business, you need to understand it well and a failure to do so can be the difference between profit and loss, or even getting the deal done at all.

Some of the most common challenges facing a Strategic Transaction are SEC oversight to the extent that either company is publicly held, anti-trust issues if either company or a combination of both will have material market share, or industry regulators' regulations if the buyer is entering a business in which they have not previously operated.

B. The Press

Whether private or public, few companies can afford to ignore the press. The press can have a powerful impact on a company in several ways. Press reports help investors paint a picture of a company's future potential and can have substantial immediate effects on the stock price of a public company, particularly in more speculative businesses.[43] Press reports can also have indirect effects on a business by changing the way customers, partners, suppliers and employees think about the company. Customers' impression of the quality and reliability of a product can be effected by the press. For example, the "Tylenol Murders" of 1982, where seven people in the Chicago area died suddenly after taking Tylenol that had been laced with cyanide, had a dramatic impact on the sale of Tylenol. While the press certainly didn't create the product tampering, the drama with which it was reported certainly contributed to the "scare" that forced Johnson & Johnson to issue an unprecedented recall of 31 million Tylenol bottles which cost the company approximately $125 million. In the absence of widespread press coverage Johnson & Johnson could probably have avoided such a dramatic and costly step, but doing so went a long way to restoring the confidence of consumers.

Partners and suppliers can also be substantially affected by the press. A report that a company may be in financial trouble can cause partner companies to question long-term relationships and certainly may drive them to restrict financial liability. A company whose financial stability is questioned by the press may find it more difficult to get long-term agreements signed or to get trade and other financial credit extended.

Employees' behavior can also be dramatically impacted by press reports. Employees who read about financial instability in their company may start a job search or get distracted from work. Certainly union members who read about high executive compensation and perks will be less likely to support

---

[43] The biotechnology sector is rife with examples. Since a biotech companies fortunes are made and broken on the basis of a single trial result, press reports on those results can dramatically effect the stock price. An erroneous or misunderstood report can have just as dramatic an effect. For example, in September of 2003, Reuters published an article on a company called Dendreon citing a failure in a recent trial of their most important drug as if it was new information. The stock price dropped dramatically, opening 13% down from the prior days close. Luckily for Dendreon, research analysts covering the stock were quick to react with statements that the Reuters report was old news that had already been considered in the value of the stock. But even a week later, the stock had not yet recovered the loss. "Dendreon cancer drug fails to slow disease progress," Reuters, September 18,

wage and other concessions. Similarly, a Strategic Transaction can be put in jeopardy if word leaks out early to employees, particularly in a highly unionized company where such a deal could impact employee benefits.[44]

One might argue that the press is simply a channel for information that would eventually get out anyway, and that the effect of inaccurate reports will be corrected as soon as they are. Even inaccurate reports that are quickly corrected can contribute to a longer-term negative impression of the company – a reputational malaise – that takes a long time to completely evaporate. Even when reports are accurate, the timing and "spin" of news can change the impact it has on various parties.

The other side of the coin is that the press can be a valuable tool for communication. Just as stories can do damage to relationships, they can also enhance them. The press has a powerful channel, both in terms of volume of people reached and in terms of the confidence engendered in them for accuracy and lack of bias. Good communication with the press can ensure that the market gets your explanation for the benefits of a Strategic Transaction. It can also ensure that employee apprehensions are assuaged and help address concerns of partners, suppliers and customers. Good press coverage in and of itself can help bring about the benefits of a deal.

4:13 pm EDT; "Dendreon Drops on Drug News," TheStreet.com, September 18, 2003 05:22 pm EDT.
[44] During my time as a lawyer I represented a highly unionized company that was negotiating the sale of a division. Having gone through a lengthy auction process we were in deep negotiations with the leading bidder, and were likely two days away from finalizing the contract. We got word that a national newspaper was going to break the story the next morning. This would have been disastrous for our client's relations with their union since the deal hadn't been communicated to their employees. The company was insistent that it had to carefully communicate the terms of the deal to employees and give them clear assurances that their benefits and pension would be protected. They did not want employees to read about the deal in the morning paper before they had a chance to give them the full and complete picture. We were able to get the newspaper to delay the story for one day, and rushed to get the deal closed in time. The deal was finalized that night and the company was able to communicate with employees the next morning, giving them a full and positive spin on the deal just before they read the story in the morning paper. In this situation we were able to avert disaster but it was a good cautionary tale in how the press can affect a deal.

When dealing with the press, it is important to remember their incentives. Press organizations, and individual reporters make money when they are considered a valuable source of information – when their paper is bought or program is watched. There are three key components to this equation. First they must have information. Without content they have nothing to sell, and content must be real news and not just information. Ripeness is important since once information is commonly known it is no longer news. Second, the content must be accurate. False information is worse, in most cases, than no information. Third, the information must be complete and unbiased. One side of the story does not give the reader a complete picture and again can be worse than no information at all. In many cases these three goals come into conflict and the press needs to balance one against the other. If you provide the press with information that they can use, they may be willing to publish a piece that is at least somewhat weighed to your favor. Making it easy for them to get information may tip the scales in your direction, but if the information is too biased or suspect, they will refuse to run it at all. So it is often better to give the press a somewhat less biased set of information and have them use it, than to give them something so biased that they must set it aside entirely. The relationship with the press is an iterative one. Most companies deal with the press, particularly the members of the press focused on their industry, over and over again. Developing a good relationship with a member of the press over time can generate value. If you provide accurate and relatively unbiased information on a regular basis, the reporter is more likely to accept a subtle spin in your favor and certainly more likely to run stories that benefit you even if they are accurate.

Finally, when doing a Strategic Transaction you also need to consider how to communicate with various parties directly as well as through the press. In some cases it will make sense to do direct communication and in others to work through the press or public statements (particularly for public companies that have regulatory requirements to announce certain actions or transactions). Preparing a clear communications strategy and working with the press can actually enhance the value of a deal and failing to do so can do temporary and even permanent damage.

Best Selling Books

Visit Your Local Bookseller Today or www.Aspatore.com For More Information

Marketing/Advertising/PR

Inside the Minds: The Art of Advertising: CEOs from Mullen Advertising, Marc USA, EURO RSG & Others on Generating Creative & Profitable Campaigns

Inside the Minds: Leading Advertisers – Advertising CEOs from Saatchi & Saatchi, Ogilvy & Mather, Y&R and More Reveal the Tricks of the Advertising Profession

Inside the Minds: The Art of PR – CEOs from Edelman, Burson-Marsteller, Fleishman-Hilliard & More Reveal the Secrets to the Public Relations Profession

Inside the Minds: Leading Marketers–Chief Marketing Officers from GE, Coke, Verizon, FedEx, Amex & More Reveal the Secrets to Building a Billion Dollar Brand

Inside the Minds: The Art of Building a Brand – Leading Advertising & PR CEOs Reveal the Secrets Behind Successful Branding Strategies

The Best of Guerrilla Marketing – Marketing on a Shoestring Budget

Reference

Business Travel Bible – Must Have Phone Numbers, Business Resources & Maps

The Golf Course Locator for Business Professionals – Golf Courses Closest to Largest Companies, Law Firms, Cities & Airports

Business Grammar, Style & Usage – Rules for Articulate and Polished Business Writing and Speaking

ExecRecs – Executive Recommendations For The Best Business Products & Services

Living Longer Working Stronger – Simple Steps for Business Professionals to Capitalize on Better Health

Executive Adventures: 50+ Out of the Office Escapes for Business Professionals

The C-Level Test – Business IQ & Personality Test for Professionals of All Levels

The Business Translator-Business Words, Phrases & Customs in Over 65 Languages

Small Business Bible – Phone Numbers, Business Resources, Financial, Tax & Legal Info

The Small Business Checkup – A Planning & Brainstorming Workbook for Your Business

Legal

Inside the Minds: Privacy Matters – Leading Privacy Visionaries Share Their Knowledge on How Privacy on the Internet Will Affect Everyone

Inside the Minds: Leading Lawyers – Leading Managing Partners Reveal the Secrets to Professional and Personal Success as a Lawyer

Inside the Minds: The Innovative Lawyer – Leading Lawyers Share Their Knowledge on Using Innovation to Gain an Edge

Inside the Minds: Leading Labor Lawyers – Labor Chairs Reveal the Secrets to the Art & Science of Labor Law

Inside the Minds: Leading Litigators – Litigation Chairs Revel the Secrets to the Art & Science of Litigation

Inside the Minds: Leading IP Lawyers – IP Chairs Reveal the Secrets to the Art & Science of IP Law

Inside the Minds: Leading Deal Makers – The Art of Negotiations & Deal Making

Inside the Minds: The Corporate Lawyer – Corporate Chairs on the Successful Practice of Business Law

Management

Corporate Ethics – The Business Code of Conduct for Ethical Employees

The Governance Game – Restoring Boardroom Excellence & Credibility in America

Inside the Minds: Leading CEOs – CEOs Reveal the Secrets to Leadership & Profiting in Any Economy

Inside the Minds: The Entrepreneurial Problem Solver – Entrepreneurial Strategies for Identifying Opportunities in the Marketplace

Inside the Minds: Leading Consultants – Industry Leaders Share Their Knowledge on the Art of Consulting

Inside the Minds: Leading Women – What It Takes to Succeed in the 21st Century

Being There Without Going There: Managing Teams Across Time Zones, Locations and Corporate Boundaries

Technology

Inside the Minds: Leading CTOs – The Secrets to the Art, Science & Future of Technology

Software Product Management – Managing Software Development from Idea to Development to Marketing to Sales

Inside the Minds: The Telecommunications Industry – Leading CEOs Share Their Knowledge on The Future of the Telecommunications Industry

Web 2.0 AC (After Crash) – The Resurgence of the Internet and Technology Economy

Inside the Minds: The Semiconductor Industry – Leading CEOs Share Their Knowledge on the Future of Semiconductors

Venture Capital/Entrepreneurial

Term Sheets & Valuations – A Detailed Look at the Intricacies of Term Sheets & Valuations

Deal Terms – The Finer Points of Deal Structures, Valuations, Term Sheets, Stock Options and Getting Deals Done

Inside the Minds: The Ways of the VC – Identifying Opportunities, Assessing Business Models and What it Takes to Land an Investment From a VC

Inside the Minds: Leading Deal Makers – Leveraging Your Position and the Art of Deal Making

Inside the Minds: Entrepreneurial Momentum – Gaining Traction for Businesses of All Sizes to Take the Step to the Next Level

Inside the Minds: The Entrepreneurial Problem Solver – Entrepreneurial Strategies for Identifying Opportunities in the Marketplace

Inside the Minds: JumpStart – Launching Your Business Venture, Profitably and Successfully

Financial

Inside the Minds: Leading Accountants – The Golden Rules of Accounting & the Future of the Accounting Industry and Profession

Inside the Minds: Leading Investment Bankers – Leading I-Bankers Reveal the Secrets to the Art & Science of Investment Banking

Inside the Minds: The Financial Services Industry – The Future of the Financial Services Industry & Professions

Building a $1,000,000 Nest Egg – 10 Strategies to Gaining Wealth at Any Age